SPINOZA:
A TERCENTENARY PERSPECTIVE

Edited by
BARRY S. KOGAN

Hebrew Union College-Jewish Institute of Religion

28211

©HEBREW UNION COLLEGE

LIBRARY OF CONGRESS 79-90069
ISBN 0-87820-203-X

The Efroymson Memorial Lectures are
published and distributed under the terms of
the Gustave A. and Mamie W. Efroymson Lectureship
established by Dr. Clarence W. and Robert A. Efroymson
of Indianapolis, Indiana.

CONTENTS

	Page
Preface *Barry S. Kogan*	vii
Spinoza — A Three Hundred Year Perspective *Alfred Gottschalk*	1
Spinoza's Skepticism and Anti-Skepticism *Richard H. Popkin*	5
Spinoza's Thought and Modern Perplexities: Its American Career *Lewis S. Feuer*	36
Spinoza on Man's Knowledge of God: Intuition, Reason, Revelation, and Love *David Savan*	80
Concluding Remarks *Eugene Mihaly*	104

SPINOZA:
A TERCENTENARY PERSPECTIVE
THE GUSTAVE A. AND MAMIE W. EFROYMSON MEMORIAL LECTURES

TUESDAY, MAY 2, 1978 — WEDNESDAY, MAY 3, 1978

HEBREW UNION COLLEGE-
JEWISH INSTITUTE OF RELIGION
3101 Clifton Avenue, Cincinnati, Ohio 45220

PROGRAM
TUESDAY, MAY 2, 1978
SESSION I, 2:00 P.M. — SCHEUER CHAPEL

Professor Richard H. Popkin, *Washington University*
  "Spinoza's Skepticism and Anti-Skepticism"
Chairman:
  Dean Herbert Paper, *School of Graduate Studies, HUC-JIR*
Reception, 3:45 p.m. — Klau Library

SESSION II, 8:15 P.M. — SCHEUER CHAPEL

Opening Statement: President Alfred Gottschalk, *HUC-JIR*
  Professor Lewis Feuer, *University of Virginia*
    "Spinoza's Liberalism and the Perplexities of Modern Times"
Chairman: Professor Ellis Rivkin, *HUC-JIR*
Reception, 10:00 p.m. — Sisterhood Dormitory

WEDNESDAY, MAY 3, 1978
SESSION III, 11:00 A.M. — SCHEUER CHAPEL

Professor David Savan, *University of Toronto*
  "Spinoza on Man's Knowledge of God: Intuition, Reason, Revelation and Love"
Chairman: Professor Barry Kogan, *HUC-JIR*
Concluding Remarks: Professor Eugene Mihaly, *HUC-JIR*

SPINOZA: A TERCENTENARY PERSPECTIVE
Preface

By common consensus Spinoza was one of the most rigorous and original thinkers in the entire history of Western philosophy. Not only did he lay the theoretical foundations for the scientific study of the Bible and the rise of the modern liberal state, he also developed a philosophic system so comprehensive and integrated in design that it has exercised the critical faculties and religious sensibilities of reflective people ever since. But there the consensus ends. For in the three centuries since his death, Spinoza has been viewed under a remarkably wide array of perspectives; one might even say *sub specie diversitatis*.

As a Jew, increasingly alienated from the synagogue and its teachings, the young Spinoza came to be regarded as a renegade. Given the Jewish community's tenuous position in monarchist and predominantly Calvinist Holland, its leaders found much to fear in Spinoza's daring religious and political views. For the opinions he held were as offensive to the Dutch establishment as they were to its Jewish counterpart. When Spinoza eventually rejected the option of at least public silence and outward conformity, his excommunication was insured and with it the status of a pariah in the eyes of his Jewish contemporaries. Yet for many others since then he has come to represent not the renegade so much as the first secular Jew, indeed even the prototype of the European Jewish radical. For while Spinoza plainly abandoned his faith, he nevertheless pursued his subsequent course without choosing to convert.

As a philosopher, too, Spinoza was at first almost universally condemned as an outright atheist. In fact, he continued to be denounced regularly for what Hume was to call his "hideous hypothesis" for at least a century. But with the German Enlightenment there came new appraisals of his work and a different appreciation of his significance. Mendelssohn, for example, suggested that Spinoza's purely speculative writings would not have precluded his remaining an orthodox Jew, while the poet Friedrich Novalis went so far as to portray him by the now famous epithet: *gottbetrunkener Mensch*, the "God-intoxicated man." By Heine's day the evaluation of Spinoza had changed so radically that it was possible for the poet to observe, albeit with some exaggeration, that Spinoza ground the lenses through which all the philosophers of his day unknowingly viewed the world. Since that time, this extraordinary thinker has been variously depicted as a pantheistic mystic, a forerunner of pragmatism, an absolute idealist, a herald of dialectical materialism, the last of the medieval philosophers, the first modern democrat, an intellectual masochist, and perhaps the one philosopher who attained the salvation he sought. It is as if the single-vision lens Spinoza fashioned in his writings to see God or Nature more clearly as a unity turned out to be multi-focal when directed toward the thinker himself. Spinoza thus remains a fascinating and enigmatic figure.

In view of his significant place in Jewish history, his influence on generations of young Jews struggling to come to terms with science and modernity, and of course his tremendous contribution to Western thought, it was natural for the Hebrew Union College-Jewish Institute of Religion to observe the 300th anniversary of Spinoza's death. But as a seat of liberal Judaism in the modern world, the College also has a special relation to Spinoza and his enterprise. It is an heir to what we may call his positive vision. For wherever freedom of inquiry exists to encourage the critical study of the Bible and Israel's past in conjunction with reasoned reflection about God, man, and the natural world, Spinoza's legacy remains alive.

In order to examine that legacy properly, Dr. Alfred Gottschalk, President of HUC-JIR, invited a committee of the faculty to organize a symposium of distinguished scholars to discuss Spinoza from a tercentenary perspective. The committee quickly agreed on the selection of Professors Lewis Feuer, Richard Popkin, and David Savan in recognition of both their valuable contributions to modern Spinoza scholarship and their ability to interpret the man and his thought to a wide audience. We were indeed fortunate to witness this unusual combination of skills during the proceedings.

The symposium opened on Tuesday afternoon, May 2, 1978, with words of welcome by Professor Herbert Paper, Dean of the School of Graduate Studies, who described the goals of the symposium and presented our guest lecturers. President Gottschalk introduced the evening session by explaining the College's long-standing interest in Spinoza and by paying special tribute to our former librarian, the late Adolph S. Oko, who assembled the College's rare and well-known Spinoza collection. The various sessions were chaired by faculty members, Herbert Paper, Ellis Rivkin, and myself.

Professor Popkin delivered the first paper of the symposium on "Spinoza's Skepticism and Anti-Skepticism." In it he provided new and valuable information about the intellectual *milieu* in which Spinoza moved and an analysis of skeptical and anti-skeptical tendencies in his writings. Focusing on the relation between these two tendencies, Professor Popkin maintained that Spinoza's radical skepticism about religion was not inconsistent with his confident and anti-skeptical claims on behalf of scientific and philosophic knowledge. On the contrary, the former complemented and even underwrote the latter.

Addressing the evening session on the subject of "Spinoza's Liberalism and the Perplexities of Modern Times," Professor Feuer took up the question of why Spinoza's thought never produced a distinct philosophical school. He argued that a variety of inconsistent positions in Spinoza's writings precluded the adoption of all of them by subsequent thinkers. He then went on to show how various figures in American intellectual life from Jefferson through Einstein reacted to or appropriated particular elements of Spinoza's total teaching. It should be noted here that the version of Professor Feuer's paper which follows has been considerably expanded from the original and includes much new material. He has also altered the title accordingly.

Professor Savan offered the third and final presentation, entitled "Spinoza on Man's Knowledge of God: Intuition, Reason, Revelation, and Love." He specifically undertook to re-examine Spinoza's conception of God or Nature and the problematic claim that God is both directly revealed to all of us, and yet adequately understood only by a kind of intellectual intuition, which few have achieved. Professor Savan maintained, contrary to widely held views, that Spinoza neither conceived of God in the way we ordinarily conceive of Nature nor even thought of Him as equivalent to the abstract notion of Being itself. Rather, he conceived of God as the concrete activity of existence expressing itself in the infinite variety and uniqueness of natural things. After supporting this thesis by text and example, Professor Savan devoted the remainder of his presentation to tracing the implications of this conception for the way in which Spinoza thought we may know God in revelation, in the experience of love, and in intellectual intuition.

Following each of the lectures there was a stimulating series of interchanges between the participants and those in attendance. Professor Eugene Mihaly, Executive Dean of Academic Affairs, closed the symposium with words of appreciation to all our guests and a few brief reflections on the roots and repercussions of Spinoza's thought in Judaism.

It is a pleasure for me at this point to thank all those who gave of their time, effort, and skill to hold this tercentenary observance — our distinguished speakers, whose excellent contributions made the symposium a truly memorable intellectual experience; President Gottschalk, who first suggested the project and encouraged our work at every stage; the members of the faculty planning committee — Dean Kenneth Ehrlich, Professors Eugene Mihaly, Herbert Paper, Alvin Reines, Ellis Rivkin, and Herbert Zafren — who developed the entire program and saw to its implementation; Mrs. Jessica Baron and Mrs. Ruth Frenkel and her staff, for arranging both accomodations for our guests and a lovely reception for all those in attendance. Finally, I would like to express my special thanks to Professor Mihaly for his support in helping me to prepare these lectures for publication.

It is my hope that these lectures will add valuable new perspectives to the scholarly literature focusing on Spinoza at this time, particularly in terms of his intellectual biography, his impact on the achievements and dilemmas of modern liberalism, and his significance as a philosopher of religion. New studies in all of these areas should be encouraged. Perhaps, too, the College can be of assistance to scholars in these and other areas of Spinoza research through its considerable library holdings. But most of all, I hope that these lectures will engage that wider public of nonspecialists, who value the "excellent things" about which Spinoza taught and who may still find much to learn from a man whose life was in so many ways a meditation on the improvement of the understanding.

Iyar, 5739
May, 1979

Barry Sherman Kogan

SPINOZA - A THREE HUNDRED YEAR PERSPECTIVE
Alfred Gottschalk[*]

It is my pleasure to welcome you to this symposium which we hold on the occasion of the 300th anniversary of the death of Baruch Spinoza. I realize we are slightly late, but, I assume, people dealing with Spinoza are accustomed to see things — like the master — *sub specie aeternitatis*, from the viewpoint of eternity. And from that viewpoint, the delay shrinks into nothingness.

During the past year, scholars of many countries have paid homage to Spinoza, but there is a very special reason why Hebrew Union College honors his memory. That reason lies in the fact that for a considerable time during this century our School has been one of the world centers of Spinoza research, and I hope that this symposium reinvigorates the role we have played. The achievement of establishing Hebrew Union College as a center of Spinoza research was greatly due to the efforts of one man who deserves being remembered and praised today before we turn to our scholarly deliberations.

This man was Adolph S. Oko, the librarian of our College from 1906 to 1933. He was truly for our College what Harvard University once called one of its great librarians, "the grand acquisitor." In particular, he was responsible for enlarging the book and manuscript collections of our School to make them into one of the great Hebraica and Judaica libraries of the world. And he, too, was responsible for bring-

[*]Dr. Alfred Gottschalk is President of the Hebrew Union College-Jewish Institute of Religion and Professor of Bible and Jewish Religious Thought.

ing together, literally from the four corners of the world, those rare Spinozana which he formed into our special Spinoza collection, one of the important collections of this kind in existence.

Oko was not a philosopher. When he died in 1944, he did not leave books he had written or manuscripts he had prepared dealing with the philosophy of Spinoza. His passion was to gather whatever documents, manuscripts or printed items he could find that contributed to the knowledge of Spinoza's life and philosophy. He considered himself an amanuensis to scholars and scholarship. His goal was to provide them with the richest reservoir of material imaginable to explore the sublime thought of the thinker whom he adored. Oko, while no creative Spinoza scholar himself, was, however, an efficient organizer of the Spinoza scholarship of others.

A founder, in 1921, of the *Societas Spinozana*, the international Spinoza Society, he was, during the decade in which the Society existed, flourished, and creatively published, its North American representative — *moderator* and *assessor* as the Latin nomenclature of the Society designated him. The fact that in the relatively short time of its existence the Society produced such an impressive array of books was greatly due to his drive and his solicitation of funds. Working out of our School he put, if I may phrase it this way, Cincinnati on the world map of Spinoza research. It was here where he did a great deal of tireless work on his collection of Spinozana titles. Indeed, a part of the 20,000 entries which he assembled appeared posthumously as a 600 page-volume devoted to Spinoza bibliography.

Our Spinoza collection at this campus and Oko's own personal library, now at Columbia University, are living testimony of the love of a Jew for a world philosopher whose relationship to Judaism is complex, to put it mildly. In fact, it is an intriguing question, why do we, Hebrew Union College, a Jewish theological school, honor Spinoza whom the rabbis of his day had expelled from Judaism, who, in many ways, in practice and opinion, had removed himself from the religion from which he had sprung? Why, one might proceed to ask, do other religionists, Christians, for example, pay homage today to him whom the churches denounced as *atheissimus?* Trying to answer these questions means writing the history of Spinozism. All I can do is venture an impression.

The history of Spinozism is filled with strong, and even vicious, attacks on Spinoza, the atheist and the corrupter of human morality and civility. At the same time, becoming increasingly stronger, there runs a different trend: philosophers and religious thinkers of all faiths pronouncing Spinoza one of the truly humane and pious voices of mankind: Benedictus de Spinoza, during his lifetime and later often denounced as *Maledictus*, becoming *Benedictus*-Baruch, the praised-one again. Friedrich Schleiermacher, the great Protestant theologian and religious philosopher, stated that "in sacred innocence and deep humility, Spinoza was replete with religion and filled with the sacred spirit." The greatest Spinoza researcher of this century, Stanislaus Dunin-Borkowski, a Catholic priest, devoted his life to exploring the meaning and the paths of Spinoza's thought, and his church gave him its *imprimatur.* Men of all religious convictions speak of Spinoza, the "God-intoxicated man." Shelley fantasized that Spinoza's Deity is "the soul of the universe, the spirit of universal imperishable love," and the German poet Novalis defined Spinozism as being "sated with divinity," Hegel who confessed that he knew of no greater philosophy than Spinoza's said, "there is no purer and more sublime morality than his." And Goethe found in him "the air of peace and tranquillity of the spirit."

Different as all of these paeans are, they have one aspect in common. Disregarding the details of Spinoza's philosophy they concentrate on the utter sublimity and divine serenity of his teachings, on the incorruptible purity of his thought, and elevate the philosopher to the rank of a moral model for any man. The only other philosopher to whom this happened was Socrates.

Matthew Arnold, never a deep thinker, nevertheless had an inkling of what propelled the controversial Spinoza into the realm of universal acclaim. "What a remarkable philosopher really does for human thought" Arnold wrote, "is to throw into circulation a certain number of new and striking ideas and expressions, and to stimulate with them the thought and imagination of his century or of after times. But to do this is not enough to make him great. To be great, he must have something in him which can influence character; he must, in short, have a noble character himself, a character *in the grand style.* This is what Spinoza had; and because he had it, he stands out from the multitude of philosophers."

Many of you, I am sure, know that the late David Ben-Gurion, Prime Minister of Israel, was an ardent student of Spinoza. In his view, the ban which the rabbis of Amsterdam had pronounced upon the young Spinoza was a lasting injustice that required remedy. And for many years, he called for another Jewish court which was to revoke the judgement of the Dutch rabbinical court. The ban, which to Ben-Gurion was a permanent blemish is to most of us a mere historical wrinkle long erased by the admiration for the philosopher which has continuously grown in 300 years. Against that background of admiration, let us now pursue our critical research of Spinoza.

SPINOZA'S SKEPTICISM AND ANTI-SKEPTICISM
Richard H. Popkin*

To appreciate a major aspect of Spinoza's skepticism, that of doubt concerning religious belief, one should turn first to look at the view of one of his immediate predecessors, Isaac La Peyrère (1596-1676) who was the secretary to the Prince of Condé and a member of the avant-garde intellectuals in Paris including Hobbes, Mersenne, Gassendi, and Grotius. La Peyrère was also in touch with and friendly with the leading intellectuals in Holland and Scandinavia. By 1640 or 1641 he had written the original drafts of his two major works, *Du Rappel des Juifs* and *Prae-Adamitae*. The first was published in 1643, and the second was refused permission by Cardinal Richelieu, (even though it is dedicated to him). The *Prae-Adamitae* only appeared in 1655 when it was printed in Amsterdam by Elizivier, apparently with the encouragement and/or assistance of the recently abdicated Queen Christina of Sweden.[1]

La Peyrère, who had been raised as a Protestant in Bordeaux, was accused of many intellectual and theological crimes including those of being an atheist, a Jew, etc.[2] His theology is highly philo-Semitic *and also* highly critical of certain central claims of traditional Christianity and Judaism. Among the many claims he made that were considered heretical were: that Moses did not write the Pentateuch; that as of the present moment we do not have an accurate or exact text of the Bible; that Scripture is solely the history of the Jews, not of the whole human race; that there were men (and women) before Adam, probably millions of them; that the world may have been going on for an indefinite length of time; that the significant human history is that of the Jews; that the Flood was only a local deluge in Palestine and

*Dr. Richard Popkin is Professor of Philosophy at Washington University.

did not affect the rest of the world. In addition, La Peyrère contended that the general framework of Jewish history was the election of the Jews running from Adam to Jesus; the rejection of the Jews, running from Jesus' day to the mid-17th century, and the recall of the Jews that is about to take place, when the Messiah expected by the Jews arrives and establishes His Kingdom centered on the Jewish Kingdom to arise in Palestine. (The Messiah will be assisted in all of this by the King of France.) In La Peyrère's picture of the Messianic age everybody will be saved regardless of what they may have believed.

Among the basic skeptical points La Peyrère raised were the challenge to the Mosaic authorship of the Bible and to the accuracy of the Scriptural text. To justify his deviant reading of the Biblical text, La Peyrère had to challenge the status of the accepted text. How do we know that Moses really is the author of the Pentateuch? "It is so reported, but not believed by all."[3] La Peyrère presented as *his* evidence for not believing it, evidence that was to be the basis for modern Bible criticism, the conflicts and repetitions in the text. He also raised the point, raised centuries earlier by R. Abraham Ibn Ezra, that Moses presumably could not have written the section about the death of Moses. So La Peyrère concluded,

> I need not trouble the Reader much further to prove a thing in itself sufficiently evident, that the first five books of the Bible were not written by Moses, as is thought. Nor need any one wonder after this, when he reads many things confus'd and out of order, obscure, deficient, many things omitted and misplaced, when they shall consider with themselves that they are a heap of Copie confusedly taken.[4]

This is a monumental claim, since the supposed ultimate guarantee of revealed data is that we have received it from Moses who received it from God himself. Once the connection with Moses is broken, then a really serious skepticism with regard to Judeo-Christian knowledge claims can follow. Once it is doubted that Moses was the Biblical author, then who else was? And what authority did this non-Mosaic author have to guarantee the truth of what he wrote?

The challenge to the authenticity of the Biblical text has similar skeptical results. If the authenticity of one passage is doubted, then by what criterion is one justified in accepting any other passage? La Peyrère claimed that Scripture was inaccurate in asserting that Adam was the first man, and inaccurate in asserting that everyone now on the surface of the earth is a descendant of one of the eight survivors of Noah's Flood. The basis for the charges of Scriptural inaccuracies was: first, internal evidence in the Bible that there were people who were not descendants of Adam, like Lilith and Cain's wife; second, evidence from pagan histories in relation to Biblical history; and third, evidence from the recent discoveries of peoples and cultures all over the world who have had no relation or contact with the Biblical world.

La Peyrère had developed his skeptical case as a way of justifying his own Messianic theory about the coming of the Jewish Messiah and the recall of the Jews. It is possible that he did not see the skeptical implications of what he was saying. However, when the book appeared his critics strongly pointed them out. In Holland the government condemned the book as scandalous, false, against God's Word, and a danger to the State.[5] The Bishop of Namur, where La Peyrère was then living, condemned the author "as a Calvinist and a Jew."[6] Refutations began to appear all over Europe charging La Peyrère with the temerity of challenging the whole Jewish and Christian traditions. His friend, the younger Bible critic Richard Simon casually said to La Peyrère, " it seems to me that your reflections are to ruin entirely the Christian religion."[7] The writer of Catholic encyclopedias, Louis Ellies Du Pin, said, "Of all of the paradoxes that have been advanced in our century [the seventeeth] there is not one, in my opinion with more temerity, nor more dangerous, than the opinion of those who have dared to deny that Moses was the author of the Pentateuch."[8] Ellies Du Pin and lots of others saw the kind of skepticism about revealed religion that would result, and they regarded it as the greatest skeptical menace of the time.

A leading religious skeptic of the next century, Tom Paine, spelled out the basic and important skepticism of denying the Mosaic authorship of the Pentateuch. "Take away from *Genesis* the belief that Moses was the author, on which only the strange belief that it is the word of God has stood, and there remains nothing of *Genesis*, but an anonymous book of stories, fables and traditionary or invented absurdities or downright lies."[9]

On the other hand a Jewish controversialist who argued against both Tom Paine and Joseph Priestley, among others, one David Levi, asserted that "if a Jew once calls in question the authenticity of *any part* of the Pentateuch, by observing that one part is authentic, i.e. was delivered by God to Moses, and that another part is not authentic, he is no longer accounted a Jew, i.e. a true believer." Further, Levi went on to insist that every Jew is obliged "to believe that the whole law or five books is from God" and was delivered by him to Moses. Both Jews and Christians should believe this, for "if any part is but once proved spurious, a door will be opened for another and another without end."[10]

It's difficult to determine if La Peyrère was aware of the fantastic skeptical potential of his ideas. Before connecting him with Spinoza, I just want to sketch briefly the rest of his career. In 1656, the year of Spinoza's excommunication, La Peyrère was arrested in Belgium. He languished in jail[11] until he was told he would be released if he personally apologized to the Pope for his heresies, and turned Catholic. He went to Rome, presented the Pope with a very hypocritical apology, abjured his previous views and joined the Catholic Church. La Peyrère blamed his views on his Calvinist upbringing, but insisted that there was nothing in science or reason against his views. The only objection his opponents could bring up was that all the authorities in the Jewish and Christian tradition ancient and modern were opposed to his views. This was not enough to impress La Peyrère until he learned that the Pope said he was wrong. If the Pope said so, he would accept this and abjure all the propositions in his book (over one hundred) that the Pope said were wrong. "His wish shall be my reason and my law."[12]

The Pope was so pleased with La Peyrère and his recantation that he offered him a benefice in Rome.[13] La Peyrère refused and returned to Paris, where he became the Prince of Condé's librarian and a lay member of the pious order of the Oratorians. There he spent the rest of his life, collecting more evidence for his pre-Adamite theory, and writing books that could not be published.[14]

After La Peyrère died one of his friends wrote as his epitaph,

> Here lies La Peyrère, that Good Israelite,
> Hugenot, Catholic, finally Pre-Adamite.
> Four religions pleased him at the same time,
> And his indifference was so uncommon
> That after eighty years, when he had to make a choice,
> The good man departed and did not choose any of them.[15]

La Peyrère had a great influence in the development of religious skepticism. He influenced people from Spinoza down to the mid-19th century anthropologists. A 19th century opponent, the Reverend Thomas Smyth, declared, "When, however, in modern times, infidelity sought to erect its dominion upon the ruins of Christianity, Voltaire, Rousseau, Peyrère, and their followers introduced the theory of an original diversity of human races, in order thereby to overthrow the truth and inspiration of the Sacred Scripture."[16]

La Peyrère's influence on Spinoza is indicated first by the fact that Spinoza owned a copy of the *Prae-Adamitae*[17] and used material from it in the *Tractatus Theologico-Politicus*.[18] There may have been direct influence since La Peyrère was in Amsterdam for six months in 1655 shortly before Spinoza was excommunicated from the Amsterdam Synagogue. So far no evidence has been uncovered to show that they met. Menasseh ben Israel, Spinoza's teacher, greatly admired La Peyrère's *Du Rappel des Juifs,* and in a work written in 1655, Menasseh indicated that La Peyrère was one of the very few who knew that the arrival of the Messiah was imminent.[19] In a book by one of Menasseh's friends, he indicated that both he and Menasseh had read the *Prae-Adamitae* before it was published, and that they wanted to have a disputation with the author. There is no evidence this took place.[20] Menasseh and his friend both wrote refutations of La Peyrère's book.[21] All of this indicates that La Peyrère's theories were known and opposed by a leader of the Amsterdam Jewish community, who was also a teacher of Spinoza.[22]

In 1655-56, La Peyrère was one of the most notorious writers of the time. One would suppose that a young intellectual rebel like Baruch de Spinoza would have been interested in finding out what all of this notoriety was about.

This is made more probable by some recent discoveries of the late Professor I. S. Révah about Spinoza's excommunication. Révah discovered that there were three excommunications in the same week in 1656 in Amsterdam, that of Spinoza, that of Juan de Prado, and that of Daniel Ribera, all of whom were friends. Prado was ten years older than Spinoza, and Ribera was the same age as the young philosopher. Prado apparently had become a free-thinker in Spain before coming to Holland. He wrote a work, which is lost, on why the law of nature takes precedence over the Mosaic Law. Records of the Synagogue's charges against Prado and Ribera have survived, but not those against Spinoza.[23] Also two refutations of Prado's book exist, which indicate its contents. Prado employed themes from La Peyrère about the eternality of the world, the priority of Chinese history to Jewish history, the contention that human history in general is older than Jewish history. Prado was accused of holding the view that although it is true that God created the universe this creation occurred thousands and thousands of years ago, and not at the period specified by the Bible.[24]

So, theses of La Peyrère seem to have been involved in the excommunication. Spinoza wrote an answer to the excommunication. This work grew until it finally became the *Tractatus*. In this work he employed material from La Peyrère to make out his challenge to the Bible. So La Peyrère may well have influenced Spinoza directly from the time of the excommunication onward.

However, La Peyrère seems to have remained a believer in his strange Messianic theories rather than becoming a skeptic about all religious knowledge. Spinoza, on the other hand, early in his career, joined with Prado in holding that "God exists, but only philosophically."[25] Spinoza's intellectual career consisted in working out the implications of that claim while also developing a total skepticism of the Academic kind against traditional religion. The religious skepticism of Spinoza is stated primarily in the *Tractatus Theologico-Politicus*, the appendix to Book I of the *Ethics*, and in some of the correspondence. It grows, I believe, out of Spinoza's contact with the ideas (and possibly the person) of Isaac La Peyrère, and of Spinoza's application of Cartesian method to revealed knowledge. The result is a devasting critique of revealed religious knowledge claims, whose influence and impact are still having an amazing effect in secularizing modern man.

While Spinoza was so skeptical of religious knowledge claims, he was at the same time completely anti-skeptical with regard to so-called "rational knowledge" in mathematics and metaphysics. Spinoza's view was the exact opposite of a fideist, like his contemporary, Blaise Pascal. Spinoza was not, however, schizophrenic in this. His view is that of many modern thinkers, applying rational or scientific methods to religion with destructive results, and refusing to apply these same methods to the scientific or rational world, which is supposed to be in some way self-justifying.

Spinoza changed the locus of truth from religion to rational knowledge in mathematics and metaphysics. He began his study with a most critical analysis of the claims for revealed religious knowledge. In the preface to the *Tractatus*, he asserted that before it could be decided if Scripture is true and divine, there should first be a strict scrutiny by the light of reason of this claim.[26] This scrutiny will show "that the Bible leaves reason absolutely free, that it has nothing in common with philosophy, in fact, that Revelation and Philosophy stand on totally different footings."[27] From this, it will follow for Spinoza, that there is no cognitive content to Revelation. And in developing this case Spinoza partly made use of La Peyrère's Bible criticism, and partly made use of the application of Cartesian method to religious questions.

Spinoza starts by analyzing a central religious notion, that of prophecy, which is defined as follows: "Prophecy or revelation is sure knowledge revealed by God to man."[28] But what kind of knowledge can this be? Everyone can possess ordinary natural knowledge. It is acquired by use of our faculties which depend upon our knowledge of God and His eternal laws. Is prophetic knowledge then a kind of secret, special knowledge that does not come through our faculties? Spinoza concluded, after analyzing the possibilities, that all the prophets except Jesus were using their imaginations. They were not setting forth cognitive information unavailable to others who just employ their God-given faculties. Asserting that the prophets gained their supposed information as the result of God's power, says nothing since all events, including human knowing, are the result of God's power.[29] Hence, "it follows from the last chapter [on prophecy] that, as I have said, the prophets were endowed with unusually vivid imaginations, and not with unusually perfect minds."[30] Spinoza suggested as well that that kind of imagination "was fleeting and inconstant."[31]

If this is so, what can one learn from prophecy? Not knowledge of natural and spiritual phenomena, since these can be learned by normal intellectual processes. And on the other hand, "imagination does not, in its own nature, involve any certainty of truth, such as is implied in every clear and distinct idea, but requires some extrinsic reason to assure us of its objective reality."[32] In this analysis Spinoza is applying the Cartesian method to Biblical knowledge, as well as using, as he does in this same chapter, some of La Peyrère's reasons for doubting the accuracy of Scriptural texts.

Prophecy, in itself, Spinoza asserted, affords no certainty. The prophets themselves had to ask for a Divine sign, according to the Bible, to be sure that they had been given a Divine message. "In this respect, prophetic knowledge is inferior to natural knowledge, which needs no sign."[33] Prophetic knowledge, at best, was only morally, not mathematically certain. This, Spinoza said, meant that the knowledge of the prophet did not follow from the perception of the thing, but rested on the signs given the prophet.[34] These varied according to the capacity and opinions of each prophet. Thus a sign that might convince one prophet would not necessarily convince another. Next Spinoza surveyed the various conflicting prophetic claims and experiences. In this Spinoza used some of La Peyrère's data to denigrate Biblical prophecy even more. "... Prophecy never rendered the prophets more learned, but left them with their former opinions, and ... we are, therefore, not at all bound to trust them in matters of intellect."[35] After examining the contentions of different prophets, Spinoza summed up his case that prophets, as such, have no special knowledge, and that God adapted revelations to the understanding and opinions of the prophets. The prophets did not know science or mathematics, and held conflicting opinions. "It therefore follows that we must by no means go to the prophets for knowledge, either of natural or of spiritual phenomena."[36]

It is interesting to note that in this attack against the value of prophecy, Spinoza was going against the mainstream of 17th century opinion. While Spinoza was so blithely reducing prophetic knowledge to mere opinion, many European theologians were commending a new and vital movement to find the key to interpreting Scriptural prophecies. Sir Isaac Newton belonged to this group that was sure that when they had found the key, the prophecies, especially in *Daniel* and the *Book of Revelation*, that had not yet been fulfilled, could be understood. Spinoza must have been aware of the great interest in prophetic interpretations that was going on around him amongst the theologians, but he showed no concern for their researches.[37]

If, on Spinoza's account, prophecy gave rise to no special knowledge, the second major element of revealed religion — miracles, yielded only misinformation and grounds for superstition. Before going into particular cases of alleged miraculous action, Spinoza challenged the very possibility of miracles in general or of any special Divine law known by any distinctively religious means. Spinoza argued instead that natural Divine law is "universal or common to all men, for we have deduced it from universal human nature,"[38] and that such law "does not depend on the truth of any historical narrative whatsoever. . . . inasmuch as this Divine law is comprehended solely by the consideration of human nature."[39] Therefore, no special law, like the Mosaic Law, has to be looked for by non-rational means. The Divine laws for human beings can be found by the study of human nature alone.

Spinoza went beyond the mild skeptical position on miracles that David Hume presented a century later. Hume contended that it was extremely improbable or implausible that any event is a miracle. Spinoza bluntly argued for the Academic skeptical view, namely that the occurrence of miracles is impossible. The universal laws of nature are decrees of God;[40] "nature cannot be contravened, but . . . she follows a fixed and immutable order."[41] There can be no exception to natural Divine order. Instead there can just be ignorance of what is going on due to our lack of knowledge regarding aspects of the Divine order. Thus, it should be obvious from a rational understanding of God and nature, that there cannot be any real miracles. If there were, the world would be without order and chaotic. Hence, we obviously cannot know God's nature and existence and providence from miracles. But we can know them from understanding the fixed immutable order of nature.[42] Once the question of miracles in general was settled, Spinoza turned to the particular miracles alleged to have happened according to the Bible.

After challenging the claims of those who have said that they have found special kinds of truths in the Bible, Spinoza, in chapter 7, turned his attack to deal with the problems of interpreting Scripture. Some people, he observed, "dream that most profound mysteries lie hid in the Bible, and wear themselves out in the investigation of these absurdities."[43] Instead of interpreting Scripture in this manner, Spinoza chose a most radical alternative, that of using the Cartesian method. "I may sum up the matter by saying that the method of interpreting Scripture does not widely differ from the method interpreting nature — in fact, it is almost the same."[44] For Spinoza the method of interpreting nature is basically the Cartesian method. What follows in Spinoza's analysis of the Bible is a combination of many skeptical points, a lot of them taken from La Peyrère, plus a Cartesian analysis of Scripture.

It should be noted that Descartes and the Cartesians were very careful to restrict the area in which the Cartesian method was useful *and* to exclude its employment in theology and religion. Descartes constantly answered charges that he was unfaithful in his religious views, by asserting that he was not dealing with religious topics, and that he accepted the views of the Catholic Church without any scruples.[45] This was the way Pascal read Descartes. He blamed him for only treating the God of the philosophers, and not the God of Abraham, Isaac and Jacob.[46]

For many generations historians of philosophy assumed that the Cartesian revolution necessarily led to an irreligious point of view. The reasons Descartes gave for rejecting Scholasticism would apply just as well to the rejection of the Judeo-Christian picture of the cosmos. However, more recent French scholars like Gilson, Gouhier and Koyré have made scholars aware of the possibility that Cartesianism and Christianity are actually compatible. Also they have argued that Descartes himself may well have been a genuine religious thinker, attempting to ally religion and the new science in a new harmonious relationship.[47]

Descartes' opponents, especially among the Jesuits and the Calvinists, saw potentially dangerous implications *if* the Cartesian method were applied to religion and theology.[48] But Descartes and his followers made no such an application, and they all insisted that they were orthodox in their religion.[49]

Spinoza was the first to take the step of applying his version of Cartesianism to theology and Scripture with such grim results. As was mentioned earlier, the first opinion of Spinoza that we know of is the claim of Prado and himself that God exists, but only philosophically.[50] If this is the case then the method for studying God would be a philosophical one, and not in terms of revelation or alleged supernatural data. Thus, Spinoza's method for studying anything is a development of the Cartesian method, and applies as well to God himself.

Spinoza examined the Bible on this basis to see if Scriptural statements agree with a rational analysis based on clear and distinct ideas of God and Nature. Since, Spinoza claimed, most matters raised in the Bible cannot be demonstrated, then they have to be interpreted in other ways, that is, philologically, historically, psychologically, in a word, in terms of scientific knowledge. This may provide an explanation of why certain items appear in the Bible, and why they are believed by some people, even though we have no way of telling if they are true. Spinoza thus quickly transformed the Bible from a source of knowledge to an object of knowledge, by employing the Cartesian criteria with regard to it. In terms of this, Scripture becomes some odd writings of the Hebrews over two thousand years ago, to be understood in this context.

If one took the Scriptural statements literally, and judged them on the basis of clear and distinct ideas of God and the laws of nature, Spinoza questioned whether this process yields any demonstrably certain or morally certain truth about reality. On these criteria the most that could be found in the Bible were basic moral truths, that could also be discovered through philosophical examination.[52]

In the very important chapter 15 of the *Tractatus*, entitled, "Theology is shown not to be subservient to reason, nor reason to theology: A definition of the reason which enables us to accept the authority of the Bible," Spinoza clearly showed the results of his analysis. First he outlined two alternatives he was going to reject, skepticism and dogmatism. Spinoza defined the skeptical view to be "that reason should be made to agree with Scripture." Such a view would deny the certitude of reason. On the other hand, dogmatism is taken to be the view that "the meaning of Scripture should be made to agree with reason."[53]

The dogmatic view Spinoza attributed to Maimonides and his followers, who were willing to alter and even violate the literal meaning of Scripture.[54] They rewrote and reinterpreted passages in order that they would meet rational standards. Spinoza insisted, almost like a fundamentalist, that every text has to be taken at face value.

It was the case that according to Spinoza's method of Scriptural interpretation there were a lot of passages in the Bible that would not make sense. Instead of changing the passages, as Spinoza accused Maimonides of doing, there was an equally dangerous possibility, that of accommodating reason to Scripture. This skeptical view would destroy all rational criteria, since reason would have to be altered to fit the non-rational text of the Bible. "Who, unless he were desperate or mad, would wish to bid an incontinent farewell to reason, or to despise the arts and sciences, or to deny reason's certitude."[55]

Spinoza resolved the problem at issue by insisting that philosophy and theology should be separated, rather than accommodated to each other. Philosophy is judged by rational standards, namely by clear and distinct ideas. Theology is judged in terms of its one meaningful achievement, the teaching of piety and obedience. Theology does not and cannot offer proofs of the truth of its prescriptions. If theology is kept to this role, it will be in accord with reason. What it then would ask people to do and believe is supported by philosophical evidence. The truth of theological recommendations will be decided by philosophy. Theology by itself cannot be considered true or false.

This leads to a type of total skepticism about theology and religion. Their propositions are not cognitive, except for those that can be supported by philosophy. There is no point in questioning, or even doubting theological or religious propositions. These mental acts are irrelevant to them. Earlier in the present century, the logical positivists declared that ethical discourse and aesthetic discourse were non-cognitive. They were not open to questions about the truth or falsity of value claims. In a like manner, Spinoza defused the power of theology and religion by removing them from philosophic (in the broad sense that Spinoza uses the term) or cognitively meaningful discussion. The sole function remaining for theology and religion was to teach people the path to salvation by obedience and not by reason. People who don't *understand* the path to salvation can be led to it in this manner.[56]

The analysis Spinoza made of Scripture, using the skeptical points of La Peyrère about its Mosaic authorship and other matters, and using the critical method of Cartesian science applied to the Scriptural documents, played a vital role in launching modern Bible criticism. Spinoza denied that there was any special message in Scripture that could not be learned by philosophical means. He maintained that much of the Bible can be better understood as dealing with Jewish history, primitive psychology, and similar subjects.

Spinoza's extension of Cartesian methodology to the evaluation of the Scriptural framework for interpreting man and his place in the universe led him to decide that the Bible had no place in the intellectual world. It was just a source of moral action for those who were not capable intellectually of finding the rational basis for human conduct.

Some of the opponents of Descartes who were sure that his theory would lead to infidelity and atheism found Spinoza proof of their fears. Henry More, for example, claimed, after he split with Descartes, that the latter's theory was just a form of infidelity. More said that he had heard that in Holland there were Cartesians who were "mere scoffers at religion, and atheistical." Then there came "Spinoza, a *Jew* first, a *Cartesian* and now an atheist."[57] The *Tractatus*, More asserted, challenged the very bases of Biblical religion.

Even before the pubication of the *Ethics*, with its complete naturalistic metaphysics, many readers realized that skepticism about revealed religion was explicit in Spinoza's writings. They realized that his way of treating the Bible would deny the importance or validity of the Judeo-Christian tradition. And the *Tractatus* along with the *Ethics* would permit a totally new perspective on human experience. What Pascal declared was the misery of man without the Biblical God, was for Spinoza instead the liberation of the human spirit from the bonds of fear and superstition.

Spinoza's skepticism about the values of the Biblical world, and his picture of how rational men would replace it, was far in advance of what mid-seventeenth century thinkers could accept. It was a pejorative insult for years to call anyone a "Spinozist." It took over a century before a person could safely say that he was a follower of Spinoza. And some of the German Enlightenment figures who did got in trouble in the late 18th century. The extremely tolerant Pierre Bayle asserted that Spinoza "was a systematic atheist who employed a totally new method." Bayle said the *Tractatus* was "a pernicious and detestable book" that contained the seeds of the atheism of the *Ethics*.

Spinoza's view regarding revealed religion cannot be called Pyrrhonian skepticism, or its theological version, agnosticism. A portion of Spinoza's case is carrying forward the doubts about the Scriptural text of La Peyrère. More of it is denying the cognitive content of the Bible in terms of prophecies, miracles, or anything else. This could be counted as negative skepticism or Academic skepticism. Spinoza did not just *doubt* the truth claims of the Bible. He *denied* them, except for their moral message. In this denial, it no longer makes sense to describe the contentions of revealed religion as being either true or false. Proof and doubt do not apply to them. The elements of traditional religion can be studied as aspects of the history of human stupidity for what they represent historically, sociologically or psychologically, but they cannot be studied in terms of their truth and falsity.

The denial of the value of revealed religion got labelled "skepticism," and the theologians were devoting their time to fighting skeptics and infidels. Probably the most common usage nowadays of the term "skeptic" is that of a religious unbeliever.[58] In this sense, and with the above qualifications, I think it just to rank Spinoza as a skeptic about religion, even though his views go well beyond mere doubt to complete denial. Yet if Spinoza was an irreligious skeptic, he was most unskeptical with regard to the areas of scientific and philosophical knowledge. As I suggested earlier, this is not a sign of inconsistency; it involves rather one of Spinoza's basic knowledge claims that applies to all subjects including religion.

It is obvious that Spinoza spent a lot of time studying Descartes' basic philosophical texts. He thus could not avoid coming in contact with skeptical ideas, and with the problems posed by the skeptics. Besides what he learned from Descartes, Spinoza was acquainted with the writings of the Greek skeptical writer, Sextus Empiricus.[59]

It does not matter how much Spinoza knew of the skeptical literature ancient and modern. His very negative view about philosophical skepticism is based on his examination of Descartes' thought in *The Principles of Descartes' Philosophy*, and the development of these points in Spinoza's other writings. When one considers how serious "la crise pyrrhonien" was in the middle of the seventeenth century, and especially how serious it was for Descartes, it is a bit surprising to see how calmly Spinoza faced it, and how simple he found it was to dispose of the problem. The question of skepticism comes up at least once in Spinoza's major works. His conception of the problem comes out clearly if one starts with *The Principles of Descartes Philosophy* (1666), and if one examines what he said in contrast to what Descartes said on the same issue.

At the beginning of the *Principles*, Spinoza left out Cartesian doubt as one of Descartes' means of searching for truth.[60] Spinoza said the effect of Descartes' method was that "he undertook to reduce everything to doubt, not like a skeptic, who apprehends no other end than doubt itself, but in order to free his mind from all prejudice."[61] Descartes, Spinoza said, hoped to discover the firm and unshakeable foundations of science, which could not escape him if he followed the method. "For the true principles of knowledge should be so clear and certain as to need no proof, should be placed beyond all hazard of doubt, and should be such that nothing could be proved without them."[62] It is the existence of such principles (and the intellectual catastrophe if there are none) that Spinoza appeals to in his skirmishes with the skeptics. I call them skirmishes because he really fights no large battles with them. What eliminates all of the Cartesian doubts is that one knows "that the faculty of distinguishing true and false had not been given to him by a supremely good and truthful God in order that he might be deceived."[63] In explaining this Spinoza made his fundamental basis of certainty clear.

> For, as is obvious from everything that has already been said, the pivot of the entire matter is this, that we can form a concept of God which so disposes us that we cannot with equal ease suppose that he is a deceiver as that he is not, but which compels us to affirm that he is entirely truthful. But when we have formed such an idea, the reason for doubting mathematical truth is removed. For then whenever we turn our minds in order to doubt any one of these things, just as in the case of our existence, we find nothing to prevent our concluding that it is entirely certain.[64]

Spinoza proceeded to set forth Descartes' theory, and in the course of the presentation made the centrality of the idea of God obvious. He contended that there was no point in arguing with people who deny that they have the idea. It is similar to trying to teach a blind man about colors. "But unless we are willing to regard these people as a new kind of animal, midway between man and brutes, we should pay little attention to their words."[65] The centrality appears again as Spinoza sets forth the propositions that make up Descartes' philosophy. The criterion of truth, "Whatever we clearly and distinctly perceive is true," follows after "God is utterly truthful and is not at all a deceiver."[66] Descartes had employed the criterion to prove that God was no deceiver.[67] For Spinoza, the idea of God precludes deception and guarantees that clear and distinct ideas are true.

In Spinoza's methodological presentation of his views, the unfinished *Treatise on the Improvement of the Understanding*, after he had set forth his method for discovering certain truth, he paused to consider the possibility that

> there yet remains some skeptic, who doubts of our primary truth and of all the deductions we make, taking such truth as our standard, he must either be arguing in bad faith, or we must confess that there are men in complete mental blindness, either innate or due to misconceptions, that is, to some external influence.[68]

The classification of the skeptic as mentally blind had already appeared in *The Principles of Descartes Philosophy*. One wonders what evidence Spinoza could have produced besides just appealing to how clear and certain various truths were to him. Spinoza was perplexed by his supposed skeptic. Such an individual could not affirm or doubt anything. He would not even be able to say that he knew nothing. He "ought to remain dumb for fear of haply supposing something which should smack of truth." If these skeptics "deny, grant or gainsay, they know not that they deny, grant, or gainsay, so that they ought to be regarded as automata, utterly devoid of intelligence."[69]

Thus far Spinoza's case is basically an *ad homimem* argument about the mentality and character of the skeptic or doubter. Spinoza has not yet taken up the skeptic's arguments, regardless of whether the skeptic can affirm or deny them. In a later section of the *Improvement of the Understanding*, Spinoza showed what is at issue. "Hence we cannot cast doubt on true ideas by the supposition that there is a deceitful Deity, who leads us astray even in what is most certain. We can only hold such an hypothesis so long as we have no clear and distinct idea."[70] When we think about the idea of God, we know that He cannot be a deceiver. We know this with the same certitude as we know that the sum of the angles of a triangle equal two right angles. Spinoza, also in the *Improvement of Understanding* turned aside the possibility that the search for truth would lead to an infinite regress. First one would seek a method, then a method for finding the method, etc. Spinoza contended that, "... In order to discover the truth, there is no need of another method to discover such a method; nor of a third method for discovering the second, and so on to infinity. By such proceedings, we should never arrive at any knowledge of the truth, or indeed, at any knowledge at all." Spinoza's answer to this is that

> ... the intellect, by its native strength makes for itself intellectual instruments, whereby it acquires strength for performing other intellectual operations, and from these operations get again fresh instruments, or the power of pushing its investigations further, and thus gradually proceeds till it reaches the summit of wisdom.[71]

In his later works, the *Tractatus* and the *Ethics*, Spinoza made his reasons for rejecting skepticism as a serious possibility in the rational world of philosophy clearer. (Spinoza actually discussed skepticism quite infrequently, and usually as an aside.) In the *Tractatus* in treating the proof of existence of God, Spinoza began, "As God's existence is not self-evident..."[72] Then a most important footnote was added at the end of the volume.

> We doubt of the existence of God, and consequently of all else, so long as we have no clear and distinct idea of God, but only a confused one. For as he who knows not rightly the nature of a triangle, knows not that its three angles are equal to two right angles, so he who conceives the Divine nature confusedly, does not see that it pertains to the nature of God to exist.[73]

At the end of this footnote, Spinoza said that when it becomes clear to us that God exists necessarily and "that all of our conceptions involve in themselves the nature of God, and are conceived through it, lastly we see that all our adequate ideas are true."[74]

On this theory one is a complete skeptic until one has a clear and distinct idea of God. Everything is confused or dubious without the idea of God. Spinoza's constant comparison was to the mathematical one, where if one did not have a clear and distinct idea of a triangle, then one would not know what other properties a triangle has. However, regarding the idea of God, the matter is far more significant since all our clear ideas "involve themselves in the nature of God," and are conceived through Him. As a consequence of knowing God, we know that all our adequate ideas are true.

Skepticism is both possible and necessary if one does not have a clear idea of God. Skepticism is not the product of arguments, but of ignorance. It does not get refuted, but is replaced by the tremendous consequences of having a clear idea of God. With such an idea there is no possibility of considering Descartes' further skeptical possibilities, that God may be a deceiver. The true and adequate idea of God eliminates that as a genuine possibility.

The skeptic might still raise the question, how do you know when you have a clear and certain, or true and adequate idea of God? The idea according to Spinoza will apparently be self-validating. It will be "so firmly and incontrovertably true, that no power can be postulated or conceived sufficient to impugn them."[sic] The person who does impugn the idea of God is just an ignoramus and does not really know what the idea is like. The person who possesses the idea will realize that it is true and cannot possibly be false no matter what skeptical arguments are introduced. One of the reasons why it cannot be false is the so-called argument from catastrophe, namely that this and everything else would become uncertain.

Near the end of Book II of the *Ethics*, Spinoza deals with skepticism in more detail, diagnosing it to be ignorance.

Proposition XLIII states, "He, who has a true idea, simultaneously knows that he has a true idea, and cannot doubt of the truth of the thing perceived."[75]

For Spinoza there is no need for a long elaborate proof against the skeptics, since he is claiming contrary to Descartes that the very act of understanding as such makes one aware that he knows and knows what he knows. If the skeptic claims that such a person could have made a mistake, Spinoza contended this would be impossible if the person in question had a clear and certain idea. This in itself would be its own criterion. As some of the quotations above show the choice for Spinoza is either that one knows God and all that follows from that knowledge or one knows nothing. Since we do, in fact, know something, such as that a triangle is equal to two right angles, a truth that shows itself in the very act of knowing it, we do not have to be bothered by skepticism. Instead we have to analyze our truth to discover what makes it true, namely God. The skeptic knows nothing as long as he has all his purported doubts. He is in a state of ignorance. This could only be cured by a genuine knowing experience. He might be in the stage of suspense of judgment, which means "that he does not perceive the matter in question adequately."[76] Presumably as soon as he does he will give up his skepticism.

Spinoza did not see skepticism as a menace to European philosophy. The quotations I have used are almost his total discussion of the matter. Unlike Descartes, who had to do battle with skepticism to arrive at dogmatic truth, Spinoza just started with an assurance that his system was true, and anyone who didn't believe this was either truth-blind [like color-blind] or an ignoramus. The latter can be helped if he can be gotten to improve his understanding and can be gotten to know something clearly and certainly or adequately.

Spinoza's epistemological dogmatism is most likely the furthest removed from the skepticism of any of the new philosophies of the seventeenth century. It is a genuine antiskeptical theory trying to eliminate the possibility or meaningfulness of doubting or suspending judgment. Spinoza began his system where others were trying to get to *after* they had succeeded in overcoming the skeptical menace. Spinoza just eliminated the skeptical position by beginning with the axiom, "A true idea *must* correspond with its ideal or object,"[77] [my italics], and then insisting that people have true ideas. The evidence for this claim is personal experience. For the former there is no evidence since it is an axiom of Book I of the *Ethics*. As an axiom it does not require the need to build bridges from ideas to objects.

According to Spinoza there are no real skeptics, only ignoramuses. With his monumental assurance, based on his clear and certain, and true and adequate idea of God, Spinoza could answer his former disciple, Albert Burgh, who had asked, "*How I [Spinoza] know that my philosophy is the best among all that have ever been taught in the world,*"[78] by saying, "I do not presume that I have found the best philosophy, I know that I understand the true philosophy."[79] If Spinoza is asked how he knows this, his answer is his usual one, the same way that he knows that the three angles of a triangle add up to two right angles: "That this is sufficient, will be denied by no one whose brain is sound, and who does not go dreaming of evil spirits inspiring us with false ideas like the true. For the truth is the index of itself and of what is false."[80]

Spinoza's complete anti-skepticism about knowledge reinforced his skepticism about religious knowledge. True knowledge is based on the true and adequate idea of God, which is clear and obvious when it is understood, it is evident that

God cannot be the figure or person represented in popular religion. God's judgment might have been claimed to transcend our understanding entirely. "Such a doctrine might well have sufficed to conceal the truth from the human race for all eternity, if mathematics have not furnished another standard of verity in considering solely the essence and properties of figures without regard to their final causes."[81] Our clear and certain ideas indicate that God has no motives, nor does He act for purposes. There are no value properties in nature that God is attempting to increase. All of the nonsense people say on these matters,

> sufficiently shows that everyone judges of things according to the state of his brain, or rather mistakes for things the forms of his imagination. We need no longer wonder that there have arisen all of the controversies we have witnessed, and finally skepticism; ... men judge of things according to their mental disposition, and rather imagine than understand; for if they understood phenomena, they would, as mathematics attest, be convinced, if not attracted by what I have urged.[82]

Thus, for Spinoza the religious controversies constructed on ignorance of the idea of God just lead to skepticism. If instead the problem is first approached through mathematical ideas, and next through knowledge of God, people will see how false and how stupid popular religion actually is. The total dogmatism of Spinoza then justifies a doubt and finally a denial of popular religions.

Spinoza believed that he had discovered a way to dispose of any force of skepticism while developing a (or *the*) completely certain system of philosophy. The God of his philosophy provided the basis for a complete skepticism toward or denial of popular religion, as well as of the theological systems of Judaism and Christianity. The God of Spinoza's system, one knows, would provide a bulwark against any skeptical challenge, since the challenge could be written off as a case of ignorance or truth-blindness. The skeptic would keep raising points like "How do you know it is true?" and Spinoza would reply that truth is the index of itself, so that question is either asked in ignorance or stupidity.

Spinoza's anti-skepticism was only challenged by one major skeptic, Pierre Bayle. For the rest of the avant-garde thinkers Spinoza's skepticism with regard to religion coupled with a dogmatic anti-skepticism about knowledge became a model, as in the case of many of the English Deists and French Enlightenment thinkers who supported the many skeptical points raised by La Peyrère and Spinoza until they reached a point where they thought they had abolished traditional religion (and tried to do it politically during the Reign of Terror). D'Holbach could, for example, argue dogmatically for a naturalistic metaphysics while writing the *Three Imposters: Moses, Jesus, and Mohammed*.[83]

Religious skepticism and dogmatic metaphysics formed the combined position of many in the Enlightenment. It was not until Hume that someone appeared who was both a religious skeptic and an epistemological one. The religious skepticism spawned by La Peyrère and Spinoza dominated the avant-farde position in England, France and later Germany. The course of a century and a half of religious skepticism gutted the usual defenses of revealed religion, and forced its adherents to argue for it in spite of the skeptical criticisms, as Hamann, Lammenais, and Kierkegaard did.

The drama of how the Western World lost its religious innocence is closely bound up with the rise and flourishing of religious skepticism, with La Peyrère's critique of the Mosaic authorship of the Pentateuch and Spinoza's full-blown attack on popular religion. As a result of these challenges, Western religion had to develop new defenses, and take on new forms, or slowly wither away.

FOOTNOTES

1. The most detailed picture of La Peyrère's life appears in Jean-Paul Oddos, *Recherches sur la vie et l'oeuvre d'Isaac La Peyrère* (1596?-1676), Thèse de 3eme Cycle, (Grenoble, 1974). See René Pintard, *Le Libertinage érudit*, pp. 355-61, 379, 399, 420-24, and 430; and R. H. Popkin, "The Marrano Theology of Isaac La Peyrère," *Studi Internazionali di Filosofia*, V (1973), pp. 97-126.
2. Early in his career, he was accused of atheism and impiety, but was acquitted by the French Reformed Synod. No information is known about the charges. Cf. Bibliothèque Nationale Ms. Fonds Francais 15827, fols. 149 and 162.

   See the interpretations of Don Cameron Allen, *The Legend of Noah*, (Urbana, 1963), pp. 86-90 and 130-37; David R. McKee, "Isaac de la Peyrère, a Precursor of the 18th Century Critical Deists," *Publications of the Modern Languages Association*, LIX (1944), pp. 456-485: and Pintard, *Le Libertage érudit*, pages cited in Note 2.
3. La Peyrère, *Men before Adam*, Book III, chap. 1, pp. 204-5. Since there are several different printings of *Prae-Adamitae*, it does not help to give the references to the original. They can easily be found since the chapter order is the same in the English translation as in the Latin original.
4. *Ibid.*, Book III, II, chap. 1, p. 208.
5. Condemnation of the President and Council of Holland/Zeeland, The Hague, November 26, 1655, The British Library has a copy of this document.
6. La Peyrère's *Lettre à Philotime*, pp. 123-24. Also the work was condemned at Rome and Paris. Cardinal Grimaldi said it was "un livre tres pernicieux [parce] que le doctrine qu'il contient est damnable, contraire a la parole de Dieu and a l'Escripture Sainte," Bibl. Nat. Coll. Baluze 325, fol. 63-66.

   La Peyrère's friend, Gilles Ménage, asked him to send him the book "avant qu'il fût mis enlumière," *Menagiana*, (Paris, 1729), Tome III, p. 68.
7. Letter of Richard Simon to La Peyrère, in Simon, *Lettres choisies de M. Simon*, (Rotterdam, 1702), Tome II, pp. 12-13.
8. Louis Ellies du Pin, *Nouvelle Bibliothèque des Auteurs Ecclesiastiques*, Seconde edition, (Paris, 1690), Tome I, p. 4.
9. Thomas Paine, *The Age of Reason, Part the Second, Being an Investigation of True and Fabulous Theology*, (London, 1795), p. 14.
10. David Levi, *Letters to Dr. Priestley in answer to his Letters to the Jews, Part II, occasioned by Mr. David Levi's Reply to the Former Part*, (London, 1789), pp. 14-15.
11. R. Popkin, "Marrano Theology," p. 107 and notes 73 and 74. While he was in jail a Papal letter declared La Peyrère was "un heritique detestable." Cf. La Peyrère, *Letter à Philotime*, p. 130.

12. *Ibid.*, pp. 42-43.
13. La Peyrère, *Lettre à Philotime*, pp. 142-168.
14. Cf. Richard Simon's six letters to La Peyrère, *Letters choisies*, II, pp. 1-23, the letter to M.Z.S., pp. 24 ff, and IV, pp. 36-45. See also Michel de Marolles, *Le Livre de Genese*, (n.p, n.d); and the manuscript at Chantilly in the Prince of Condé's collection, No. 191 (698).
15. Cited in Gilles Ménage, *Menagiana* (Paris and Amsterdam, 1715), Vol. III, p. 69.
16. The Reverend Thomas Smyth, *The Unity of the Human Races proved to be the Doctrine of Scripture, Reason and Science*, (Edinburgh, 1851), p. 35.
17. See the list of Spinoza's books in Jacob Freudenthal, *Die Lebensgeschichte Spinoza's*, (Leipzig, 1899), Item 54 is "Praeadamitae, 1655."
18. For a list of some of the borrowings, see Leo Strauss *Spinoza's Critique of Religion*, (New York, 1965), pp. 264 and 327. Chapter three of this study is devoted to analyzing La Peyrère's contribution, concluding as I and Hans Joachim Schoeps (in *Philosemitismus in Barok*, (Tubingen 1952), pp. 3-18) do, that La Peyrère's theory is basically that of a Marrano, i.e., a Jewish convert to Christianity, and that La Peyrère was probably himself a Marrano.
19. Menasseh ben Israel's letter of Feb. 1, 1655, published in Paul Felgenhauer's *Bonum Nuciam Israeli quod offertur Populo Israel and Judae in hisce temporibus novissimus de MESSIAH*, (Amsterdam, 1655), pp. 89-90.
20. See the "Beschluss" to Felgenhauer's *Anti-Prae-Adamitae*, pp. 89-90.
21. Felgenhauer's is the *Anti-Prae-Adamitae* identified in the previous footnote. In it Felgenhauer argued that only Jesus was a pre-Adamite, since he was before all men and after them.

    Menasseh ben Israel listed in his *Vindiciae Judaeorum* (London, 1656), in his works that are "ready for the Presse," p. 41, *Refutatio libri qui titulus Praeadamitae*. This work never appeared and no manuscript has been found.
22. Cf. Popkin, "Menasseh ben Israel and Isaac La Peyrère," *Studia Rosenthalia*, Vol. VIII pp. 59-63.
23. I. S. Révah, "Aux Origines de la rupture spinozienne: Nouveaux documents sur l'incroyance d'Amsterdam a l'époque de l'excommunication de Spinoza," *Revue des etudes juifs*, Tome III (XXIII) (1964), pp. 370-73 and 391-408.
24. I. S. Révah, *Spinoza et Juan de Prado*, (Paris, The Hague, 1959), esp. pp. 84-153.
25. Révah, *Spinoza et Juan de Prado*, p. 43.
26. Benedictus de Spinoza, *Opera quotquot reperta sunt*, ed. J. Van Vloten and J. P. N. Land, Tomus secundus, (The Hague, 1914), *Tractatus Theologico-Politicus*, p. 89; English translation of R.H.M. Elwes, *The*

Chief Works of Benedict de Spinoza, Vol. I, (New York, 1955), *Tractatus,* p. 8.

27. Elwes translation, p. 9; Latin text, p. 90.
28. Elwes translation, p. 13; Latin text, p. 93.
29. Elwes translation, p. 25; Latin text, p. 106.
30. Elwes translation, p. 27; Latin text, p. 107.
31. Elwes translation, p. 25; Latin text, p. 107.
32. Elwes translation, p. 28; Latin text, p. 108.
33. Elwes translation, p. 28; Latin text, pp. 108-09.
34. Elwes translation, pp. 29-30; Latin text, pp. 110-111.
35. Elwes translation, p. 33; Latin text, p. 113.
36. Elwes translation, p. 40; Latin text, p. 120.
37. This school of English and Dutch theologians was given its theoretical foundation in Joseph Mede's *Clavis Apocalyptica,* (Cambridge, 1632). Many important English theologians including Sir Isaac Newton, in his *Observations upon the Prophecies of Daniel, and the Apocalypse of St. John,* (London, 1733) and William Whiston, Newton's successor, followed the interpretative framework laid down by Mede.
38. Elwes translation, p. 61; Latin text, p. 137.
39. Elwes translation, p. 61; Latin text, pp. 137-38.
40. Elwes translation, p. 83; Latin text, p. 158.
41. Elwes translation, p. 82; Latin text, p. 157.
42. Elwes translation, p. 85; Latin text, pp. 159-60.
43. Elwes translation, p. 99; Latin text, p. 172.
44. Elwes translation, p. 99; Latin text, p. 172.
45. See, for instance, Descartes' letter to the Doctors of the Sorbonne, prefixed to the *Meditations,* entitled "To the most wise and illustrious the Dean and the Doctors of the Sacred Faculty of Theology," Haldane-Ross, Vol. I, pp. 133-137; A. T., Vol. VII, pp. 1-6.
46. Pascal, *Oeuvres completes,* (Paris, 1963) preface by Henri Gouhier, and noted of Louis Lafuma, "Le Memorial," p. 618. "Dieu d'Abraham, Dieu d'Isaac, Dieu de Jacob, non des philosophes et des savants."
47. Cf. Etienne Gilson, *Etudes sur le role de la pensée médievale dans la formation du système cartésian,* and *La Liberté chez Descartes et la theologie;* Henri Gouhier, "La Crise de la theologie au temps de Descartes, and *La Pensée religieuse de Descartes;* and Alexandre Koyré, *Essai sur l'idee de Dieu et les preuves de son existence chez Descartes.*
48. See, for example, the criticisms of Descartes by the Jesuit Father Bourdin and by the Calvinists, Martinus Schook and Gisbert Voetius. Bourdin's criticism appears in "Objections Leptimae, cum notis authoris A-T, Vol. VII, pp. 451-561. Schook's and Voetius' criticism appears in *Admiranda methodus novae philosophiae Renati DesCartes.*

49. Descartes' answer to Father Bourdin appears in "Objectiones Septimae cum notis authoris," A. T., Vol. VII, pp. 451-561, and Descartes' complaining letter to Father Dinet, the Jesuit Provincial, A. T., Vol. VII, pp. 563-603. His answer to Schook and Voetius is in "Epistola Renati DesCartes ad Celeberremium virum D. Gisbertum Voetium," A. T., Vol. VIII-2 (Paris, 1695).
50. Cf. Footnote 25 above.
51. Cf. Spinoza, *Tractatus*, caput. vii. "De Interpretatione Scripturae;" and caput. viii, "In quo ostenditur, Pentateuchon et libros Josuae, Judicum, Rut, Samuelis, et Regum non esse autographa, Deinde inquiritur, an eorum omnium Scriptores plures feurint, an unus tantum, et quinam." Elwes translation, pp. 98-132.
52. Elwes translation, pp. 100-101, 119, 175-81 and 186-87; Latin text, pp. 173, 190, 237-243, and 247-48.
53. Elwes translation, p. 190; Latin text, p. 250.
54. Elwes translation, pp. 114-118 and 190-191; Latin text, 186-189, and 250-251.
55. Elwes translation, p. 197; Latin text, p. 256.
56. Elwes translation, pp. 198-199; Latin text, pp. 257-258.
57. Henry More to Robert Boyle, letter of Dec. 4, [1660?], in *The Works of Robert Boyle*, ed. by Thomas Birch, (London, 1772), Vol. VI, p. 514.
58. Webster's *Third International Dictionary* gives as one of the three meanings of "skeptic," "a person marked by skepticism regarding religion or religious principles;" and one of the three meanings of "skepticism," "doubt concerning but not necessarily denial of the basic religious principles (as immortality, providence, relevation)."
59. Letter LX (LVI) to Hugo Boxel, The Hague 1674, Elwes translation, Vol. II, p. 387; Latin text, Vol. III, p. 191.
    Piero de Vona, "Spinoza e lo scetticismo classico," *Rivista critica di Storia della Filosofia*, Anno 1958, fasc. III, pp. 291-304.
60. Spinoza, *The Principles of the Philosophy of René Descartes*, in *Earlier Philosophical Writings*, translated by Frank A. Hayes, (Indianapolis, 1963), p. 13; Latin text, Vol. IV, p. 110.
61. *Ibid.*, Hayes translation, p. 13; Latin text, Vol. IV, p. 110.
62. *Ibid.*, Hayes translation, p. 13; Latin text, Vol. IV, p. 111.
63. *Ibid.*, Hayes translation, p. 17; Latin text, Vol. IV, p. 114.
64. *Ibid.*, Hayes translation, p. 20; Latin text, Vol. IV, p. 116.
65. *Ibid.*, Hayes translation, p. 33; Latin text, Scholium to Prop. VI, p. 126.
66. Spinoza, *Principles*, Part I, Prop. XIII and XIV. It is interesting that in the *Ethics* the section on God never appeals to his non-deceptive aspect.
67. Spinoza, *On the Improvement of the Understanding*, Elwes translation, Vol. II, p. 17; Latin text, *Tractatus de Intellectus Emendatione*, Vol. I, p. 14.
68. *Ibid., loc.cit.*

69. *Ibid., loc.cit.*
70. *Ibid.*, Elwes translation, p. 30; Latin text, I, p. 25.
71. *Ibid.*, Elwes translation, pp. 11-12; Latin text, I, pp. 10-11. I should like to thank Prof. J. N. Watkins of the London School of Economics for making me aware of the importance of these passages.
72. Spinoza, *Tractatus*, Elwes translation, p. 84; Latin text II, p. 159.
73. *Tractatus*, Elwes translation, p. 270; Latin text, II, p. 315.
74. *Tractatus*, Elwes translation, pp. 84-85; Latin text, II, pp. 159-60.
75. Spinoza, *Ethics*, Elwes translation, pp. 114-15; Latin text, pp. 107-08.
76. *Ethics*, Elwes translation, p. 124; Latin text, I, p. 117.
77. This is the sixth axiom to the first book of Spinoza's *Ethics*.
78. Spinoza's letter to Albert Burgh, 1675, Elwes translation, Vol. II, p. 416; Latin text, III Epistola IXXVI, pp. 232-233.
79. *Ibid.*, Elwes translation, p. 416; Latin text, III, p. 233.
80. *Ibid.*, Elwes translation, pp. 416-417; Latin text, III, p. 233.
81. Spinoza, *Ethics*, Elwes translation, p. 77; Latin text, I, p. 25. (This and the following quote are from the appendix to Book I of the *Ethics*.)
82. *Ibid.*, Elwes translation, p. 80; Latin text, pp. 71-72.
83. The final and best known version of the *Three Impostors* is attributed to Baron d'Holbach. On the *Three Impostors*, its history, and possible authors, see Don Cameron Allen, *Doubt's Boundless Sea*, (Baltimore, 1964), pp. 224-243; and Gerhard Bartsch, ed. *De Tribus Impostoribus*, (Berlin, 1960), "Einleitung," pp. 5-38.

SPINOZA'S THOUGHT AND MODERN PERPLEXITIES: ITS AMERICAN CAREER
Lewis S. Feuer*

I

Spinoza's place in the history of thought is rather anomalous. He is the only great philosopher who founded no school. There have been Cartesians, Leibnizians, Lockeans, Humeans, Kantians, Hegelians, Nietzscheans, even Berkeleyans, but in this sense, there have never been Spinozists.[1] For no one recorded in the history of ideas seems ever to have accepted all of Spinoza's major tenets.[2] Different men have selected for their use some particular doctrine of Spinoza's while rejecting the others; nobody seems to have found it possible to accept all the central ones. Many a Kantian could quite whole-heartedly affirm all of Kant's chief propositions concerning the synthetic *a priori*, the categories of the understanding, the antinomies of pure reason, and the imperatives of the practical reason. And indeed, Jewish philosophers in the nineteenth century were the chief proponents of Kant's standpoint.[3]

Why was it then that a Spinozist school never arose as did, for instance, a Kantian one? The answer seems to me to lie primarily in the fact that Spinoza's philosophy, unlike Kant's, was much more evidently a system of propositions with profound inconsistencies, a system in a logically unstable equilibrium, vulnerable at several *loci*. Here was a thinker who said God was Nature, and that the laws of

*Dr. Lewis Feuer is University Professor of Sociology and Humanities at the University of Virginia.

His nature were to be grasped by the geometrical method, but who also said that numbers were only aids to the imagination, and not the basis for the truths of reason: how then could any law of nature be regarded as part of our rational understanding of God's nature?[4] Spinoza the mystic was incompatible with Spinoza the scientist. Here was a thinker who, because he affirmed a psychophysical parallelism — that the order of mental modes corresponded to that of the physical modes — was consequently obliged to assert that the human mind can be no more immortal or eternal than its corresponding brain tissues and occurrences. Nonetheless, contravening his own propositions, Spinoza declared: "Nevertheless, we feel and know by experience that we are eternal." But how could Spinoza introduce a feeling into his philosophical geometry? Here was a thinker who bade us accept the doctrine of determinism, and to love the God from whose nature "infinite numbers of things" followed in "infinite ways," the God who could fashion the varieties of men from Albert Einstein to Adolf Hitler. The same thinker told us that "the mass of mankind remains always at about the same pitch of misery, . . . [and] is always best pleased by a novelty which has not yet proved illusive," a trait that "has been the cause of many terrible wars and revolutions."[5] But would not these infinite modes of horror lead us to an intellectual hatred of God rather than to an intellectual love of Him, for God Himself would, despite Spinoza's dialectical efforts, be the cause of evil.

Spinoza himself could scarcely take delight in the varieties of human evil and folly as exhibiting the infinitude of God's power. His own moral intuitions were at odds with his metaphysics. No contemporary event more deeply affected Spinoza than the brutal lynching in 1672 of John de Witt, the Grand Pensionary of Holland, whom Spinoza admired as the rational statesman of his time. As he told Leibniz, Spinoza wished to go out into the street bearing a placard with the words *ultimi barbarorum* (lowest of barbarians), and to confront the murderous mob.[6] Spinoza's landlord, knowing that Spinoza would likewise be torn to pieces, barred the door. Yet Spinoza, re-reading his own *Ethics*, would have had to say: "God's power shows itself in infinite ways, realizing all things that can be conceived by infinite intellect, and one of them is the lynching by barbarians of a free spirit." In Spinoza's own words: "Because to Him material was not wanting for the creation of everything, from the highest down to the very lowest grade of perfection."[7] As a naturalistic political philosopher, furthermore, Spinoza would have had to say: "The mob has more power, hence more right, as well as more of God's power than the free man, de Witt; hence, it is right that they lynch him if they would." But the moral convictions of Spinoza, the free man, scarcely accepted such a proposition. If he felt despite his geometrical metaphysics that "we feel and know by experience that we are eternal,"[8] his action also seemed to say: "Despite my naturalistic equation of right with power, I feel and know by experience that such actions are wrong, and I cannot believe that the infinite nature of God requires an infinite variety of human cruelties." Spinoza's concept of divine perfection, and the mandate to admire the infinite variety of all things, demands a kind of human masochism; we feel that the universe would have been more perfect without a finite mode such as Adolf Hitler, that God would have done better to actualize a second Einstein instead.

Imposing though the architectonic of his geometrical system was, Spinoza himself harbored doubts concerning the logical cogency of his demonstrations. The next to the last proposition of the *Ethics* is the most unusual for a book composed according to the mathematical method: "Even if we did not know that our mind is eternal, we should still consider as of primary importance Piety and Religion, and absolutely everything which in the Fourth Part we have shown to be related to strength of mind and generosity."[9] What would one think of a theorem in a textbook of geometry that said that even if an entire successive batch of theorems proved to be invalid, that would not affect the validity of the theorems already demonstrated in previous sections? Such a theorem would indeed be equivalent to the assertion that a whole batch of propositions was logically independent of its predecessors, for the proof of the logical independence of two propositions, a and b, consists precisely in showing that both the proposition a and its contradictory are equally consistent with b. To this extent, Spinoza's system is not one whose parts are completely interdependent; its "unity" is usually overestimated, for, as Spinoza says, all that he writes about the intellectual love of God might be false without affecting the truth of his psychological propositions concerning the hedonistic, free man.

One wonders if other components of Spinoza's system are similarly a-systematic. Here is Spinoza, a determinist, who yet writes a book on the ethics of the free man, as well as a treatise and a half advising him as to what political measures might advance the lot of free men. Presumably the free man can then act upon the prescriptive advice, although the multitude lacks this power of free action: "Experience, however, teaches us but too well, that it is no more in our power to have a sound mind, than a sound body."[10] Free men have the power to act freely, and to adopt Spinoza's ethical and political principles; if so, this act seems to be a choice on their part, for if they are simply determined in accordance with psychophysical laws to do so, they should be no more admired than the wretch who inevitably destroys himself according to those same laws. Might God's infinite power, we suggest, manifest itself in the existence of a variety of men who have varying degrees of freedom from the governance of strict determinist laws? Is it an "inadequate idea" on Spinoza's part that he can define God's power as expressing itself only in a determinist order rather than in one with domains of indeterminacy and freedom?

The unity of Spinoza's system was thus only an apparent one; it conjoined a variety of disparate themes and ideas. Each of Spinoza's themes might at some time, under specific historical and personal circumstances, be appropriated by some group of thinkers; at the same time, they would reject much else that a disciple would have regarded as equally essential to Spinoza's philosophy. Spinoza said he did not wish to create a school "named after him."[11] This wish was fulfilled. But if he never encouraged that species of mental bondage that characterizes the master's disciples in a "school" of thought, Spinoza was of that company such as Locke and John Stuart Mill who helped men in diverse ways to achieve their own freedom.

Thus, Spinoza's philosophy has been used in the most contrary ways in the history of ideas. American transcendentalists drew on Spinoza's pantheism, his notion of an all-encompassing God, but they found his determinism repellent. Justice Holmes found congenial Spinoza's view of Nature as a system of contending forces, but he had no use for Spinoza's logical machinery, his postulates concerning God, substance, and modes. Horace M. Kallen was attracted to Spinoza as the theorist of the dynamic of nature's energies, but he could never ground his faith in the free individual in Spinoza's determinism. By contrast, though Walter Lippmann saw a deep wisdom in Spinoza's conception of the free man, his theology was repugnant to Lippmann's agnostic spirit. The sociological careers of Spinoza's ideas were the outcome of a socio-historical selection in which strangely enough the character of Spinoza, the excommunicate rebel, was far more potent than his formal arguments.

II

It is a curious fact, to begin with, that Spinoza failed to influence in any way the intellectual spokesman of the American Revolution. Not that his works were unknown. The philosophic Quaker merchant of Philadelphia, James Logan, possessed, for instance, in his library during the first part of the eighteenth century, a copy of Spinoza's *Tractatus Theologico-Politicus*.[12] Jefferson himself moreover had gone to the trouble of purchasing the original edition of Spinoza's *Opera posthuma,* published in Amsterdam, in 1677, as well as the original translation into English of Spinoza's *Tractatus Theologico-Politicus,* published in London in 1689. They were among the volumes he later sold to the Library of Congress.[13] Thomas Jefferson thus knew Spinoza's ideas, but Jefferson felt evidently there was nothing in common between his conception of "inalienable rights" and Spinoza's notion of "natural right." As Jefferson wrote to his old friend and political opponent, John Adams, in 1823:

> . . . I can never join Calvin in addressing *his God*. He was indeed an atheist, which I can never be; or rather his religion was daemonism . . . Now one-sixth of mankind only are supposed to be Christians; . . . This gives completely a *gain de cause* to the disciples of Ocellus, Timaeus, Spinoza, Diderot and D'Holbach. The argument which they rest on as triumphant and unanswerable is, that in every hypothesis of cosmogony, you must admit an eternal pre-existence of something . . . They say then, that it is more simple to believe at once in the eternal pre-existence of the world, as it is now going on, . . . than to believe in the eternal pre-existence of an ulterior cause, or Creator or the world, . . . On the contrary, I hold . . . that when we take a view of the universe, . . . it is impossible for the human mind not to perceive and feel a conviction of design, consummate skill, and indefinite power in every atom of its composition.[14]

Jefferson in this passage, perhaps the only one in which he explicitly discussed Spinoza's philosophy by name, associates Spinoza's thought with that of the eighteenth-century French materialistic atheists, Diderot and D'Holbach. The latter, disbelievers in the argument from design for the existence of a Creator, simply accept the existence of the world as a *causa sui*. Such a philosophy could never provide Jefferson with a basis for his own theory of "inalienable rights," for men, according to Jefferson, are "endowed by their Creator" with the inalienable rights to life, liberty, and the pursuit of happiness. And if a Creator were not to exist, then the notion of Creator-endowed inalienable rights would collapse. Only on a theistic basis does the notion of "inalienable rights" make any sense. Otherwise all "rights" are sociologically alienable; rulers have decreed that men should be deprived of their lives, liberties, and possibilities for happiness. Whenever these actions, even if recognized as legal, are said to violate inalienable human rights, that is because some higher law has presumably endowed the human individuality with rights inseparable from it.

Spinoza was the most eloquent advocate of freedom of thought and speech in the seventeenth century. His argument was, however, essentially a pragmatic, utilitarian one. It would be the state's greatest misfortune, he declares, for it to try to punish its most "enlightened" citizens, and destroy "its highest examples of tolerance and virtue." Like John Stuart Mill, Spinoza argued that "such freedom is absolutely necessary for progress in science and the liberal arts," and that it is contrary to the state's own interests for it to drive "upright" men into becoming conspirators against itself.[15] Proudly Spinoza, a Dutch patriot, adduced his empirical evidence for the utility of freedom of thought and speech:

> The city of Amsterdam reaps the fruit of this freedom in its own great prosperity and in the admiration of all other people. For in this most flourishing state, and most splendid

city, men of every nation and religion live together in the greatest harmony, ... His religion and sect is considered of no importance: for it has no effect before the judges in gaining or losing a cause, ...[16]

The Jeffersonian radical, on the other hand, finds pitfalls in Spinoza's theory of "natural right." For Spinoza makes right not only coextensive but synonymous with power. Hence Spinoza is obliged to concede that the state "has the right to rule in the most violent manner, and to put citizens to death for very trivial causes..."[17] It might seem that men have at least a natural right to freedom of speech, for as Spinoza says, "it is impossible to deprive men of the liberty of saying what they think."[18] Yet this is precisely what a totalitarian state undertakes to do, and indeed, they have done so with considerable success. Thus, on Spinoza's premises, it would follow that no natural right of Soviet dissidents to dissent has been suppressed because, as a matter of fact, that suppression was for many years successful.

Spinoza's own moral and political feelings cry out against this equation of "right" with "power," and its consequences. Nonetheless, his formal political doctrine makes it impossible for him to deny that a totalitarian regime has the "right" to suppress the majority. Doubtless he would argue that it was following a mistaken and self-defeating policy in so doing, but no "right to revolution" would develop upon the suppressed majority. "It is true," Spinoza acknowledges, "that the sovereign has the right to treat as enemies all men whose opinions do not, on all subjects, entirely coincide with its own; but we are not discussing its strict rights, but the proper cause of action."[19] Hardly a stirring argument, it would have contributed no moral force to the *Declaration of Independence*. Jefferson sought for an ethically ultimate "right to revolution," not for admonitions to the British king on the expedient exercise of power. Jefferson affirmed: "that whenever any form of government becomes destructive of these ends [life, liberty and the pursuit of happiness], it is the right of the people to alter or abolish it..."

Spinoza, by contrast, is a scientific democrat, not an ideological one. An ideological democrat is one such as Jefferson, who finds a natural virtue in the people, and who regards their revolutionary act as justified when such is their will. But Spinoza could never bring himself to any high admiration for the "people." The masses of men were, in Spinoza's eyes, irrational. "[M]an's natural passions are everywhere the same," writes Spinoza. "[T]he mass of mankind remains always at about the same pitch of misery,... Men are more led by blind desire than by reason."[20]

John Locke, Spinoza's younger contemporary, has been called the philosopher of the "Glorious Revolution" of 1688, and Jefferson's Declaration was indeed, as distinguished scholars have shown, a Lockean document.[21] To Spinoza, however, every revolution was inglorious. A successful revolution, to Spinoza's mind, would contravene the laws of social psychology: "peoples have often changed their tyrants, but never removed them or changed the monarchical form of government into any other." Of this truth, the English revolution led by Oliver Cromwell in the mid-seventeenth century was "a terrible example." "They [the English] sought how to depose their monarch under the form of law, but when he had been removed, they were utterly unable to change the form of government, and after much bloodshed only brought it about, that a new monarch should be hailed under a different name..." Furthermore, Spinoza felt that revolutions had led the peoples who made them to provoke European wars. For men brooding in guilt over their king whom they had killed would be apt to alleviate their self-directed aggression by re-directing it toward an external foreign people. As Spinoza stated it, to "divert" the people's mind "from brooding over the slaughter of the king," Cromwell's government had provoked a foreign war, thus accomplishing "nothing for the good of the country."[22]

Among our contemporaries Solzhenitsyn's outlook toward revolution is probably closest to Spinoza's. For in the judgment of the courageous Russian novelist, the Bolshevik Revolution replaced one tyranny by another that was worse, and then by aiming to establish Communist dictatorships everywhere, contributed to the collapse of European reason and the liberal democratic governments, that made the triumph of Hitler inevitable. Probably, however, there was also a strong Jewish ingredient in Spinoza's antipathy to revolution. The Jewish people and their philosophers have usually stood for stability, and dreaded the instability of mass movements. A mass people's movement generally portended for the Jews violence, massacres, lootings, persecutions, ruinations, and expulsions. No doubt Spinoza himself, at the age of sixteen, had witnessed the arrival at the Amsterdam Synagogue of the refugees from the Chmielnicki Massacre of 1648; at least one-third of Poland's Jews had perished therein. Stable authority guaranteed at least the minimal conditions of survival, whereas a movement of the masses harbored all varieties of unreason.

Spinoza's democratic political standpoint thus bore a Dutch-bound impress; provincial in its setting, it could be adopted elsewhere only under highly favorable frontier conditions; it authorized no mission for international democratic revolutions. The Netherlands fortunately had long been ruled in the towns and provinces by a commercial class without the interposition of a king. Dutch democracy thus happily arose under favored circumstances, as did later the American democracies in the colonial frontier settlements. He therefore intended his constitutional advice for those countries where a "free multitude" existed, that is, where non-democratic institutions were not established: "For a multitude that has grown used to another form of dominion will not be able without great danger to pluck up the accepted foundations of the whole dominion, and change its entire fabric."[23] Where democracy did not already exist, Spinoza counselled only that the existing political system be so directed as to ensure the welfare of the people, and the safeguarding of its "free men." Piety and obedience to God, said Spinoza, require that a man "obey the sovereign power's commands in all things;" moreover, those agitators who promote schism or revolution are probably power-seekers: "he who strives to deprive the sovereign power of such authority is aiming (as we have said) at gaining dominion for himself." The state, wrote Spinoza, "will go much faster [to ruin] if private citizens seditiously assume the championship of Divine rights."[24] According to Spinoza, one does best to work within the framework of the system one has, monarchical, aristocratic, or democratic, trying to adapt its constitution to serve the welfare of its people and the liberties of its free men.

III

According to the great French social observer and thinker, Alexis de Tocqueville, the pantheistic philosophy exerts an unusual attraction upon the citizens of a democracy. "Among the different systems by whose aid philosophy endeavors to explain the universe," he wrote, "I believe pantheism to be one of those most fitted to seduce the human mind in democratic times." "[S]uch a system, although it destroys the individuality of man, or rather because it destroys that individuality, will have secret charms for men living in democracies."[25] Certainly this generalization was validated for the generation of transcendentalists who emerged in the decade of the eighteen-thirties to exercise a profound influence on

American thought. And in their pantheon of philosophers Spinoza held well-nigh the highest place. "Spinoza has come to be revered," noted Ralph Waldo Emerson in his lecture on *Character* in 1864.[26]

Neither Spinoza's determinism nor naturalism, nor indeed his geometrical method appealed to the transcendentalists. Nor were they drawn to Spinoza's hedonism. Rather the young transcendentalists were tired of the stale Lockean-Jeffersonian materialism and Epicureanism. What drew them to Spinoza was his vision of an all-inclusive, all-comprehensive God, in whom every object, every creature from the lowliest insect to the lordliest man was a mode, a manifestation, each equally partaking of and necessary to the unity and simplicity of Substance. According to Spinoza, man above all had the privilege of achieving blessedness in an intuitive knowledge and love of God. The transcendentalists were eager eclectics; they did not hesitate to conjoin a Kantian ethic to a Spinozist base. Furthermore, if every man shared in God's power and intellect, it seemed to follow that slavery was an indignity to man's nature as a manifestation of the divine. Even if Southern spokesmen could argue plausibly that slavery was in the interests of the greatest happiness of the greatest number, slavery nonetheless stood in clear violation of the intuition of the divine ingredient in every man."[27] These "democratic philosophers," recalled Charles A. Dana in his later years, "this party of transcendental philosophers" proposed that "equality and democracy should characterize our social relations," and sought to accomplish "the reform of society ... And that was what inspired the socialist movement which began about 1835 or 1838."[28]

George Ripley, the organizing spirit in 1840 of Brook Farm, the famed Massachusetts transcendentalist colony, was much moved by Spinoza's all-embracing God. "On Sunday afternoons" at Brook Farm, "during the earlier years, Ripley elucidated Kant and Spinoza to those who cared to listen,..."[29] In 1839 Ripley was already embroiled in a public philosophic controversy in which he defended Spinoza, Schleiermacher, and De Wette against the charge of of atheism. The well-known Rev. Andrews Norton had declared that "the celebrated atheist Spinoza" was "the first writer" to hold that miracles were impossible, and to maintain that God and Nature were the same. Although Spinoza had an "affectation of religious language," Norton charged his doctrine was atheist, and the "latest form of infidelity," rampant in Germany, that was spreading to the United States: "The commotion of men's minds in the rest of the civilized world, produces a sympathetic action in our own country. We have indeed but little to guard us against the influence of the depraving literature and noxious speculation which flow in among us from Europe." Revolutions were threatening in Europe: "Long-existing forms of society are giving way,"[30] Religion, Norton argued, could not be founded on Spinoza's notion of intuitively apprehended and certain truths, but only on the authority of recorded miracles. To which Ripley replied in an anonymous pamphlet that man's soul was indeed conscious of the highest reality, and that the aspersions on Spinoza's character were cast unjustly on a "devout, sweet, unselfish, truth-seeking" man.[31]

Spinoza's thought exhilarated too the most gifted woman in America, Margaret Fuller. In 1840 Margaret Fuller, together with Emerson and Ripley, founded the transcendentalist monthly magazine *The Dial*, devoted to religion, literature, and art; it was indeed America's first genuine philosophic, critical, literary journal, the organ of an intellectual movement. Margaret Fuller in her youth had discovered Spinoza; she was 27 years old when she later discussed Spinoza's ideas with the outstanding Unitarian transcendentalist, Theodore Parker. During her editorship of *The Dial*, the famous *Conversations* that she conducted in Boston as her own unique enterprise in adult education included Spinoza among her topics, and his philosophy was a theme for her circle of friends.[32] Conservative New England thinkers, however, fearing the determinism advocated in Spinoza's philosophy, were alarmed that such a man as George Ripley was Spinoza's proponent. The leader of Vermont transcendentalism, James Marsh, president of the University at Burlington, felt that Ripley, a follower "of Spinoza" despite himself, was losing "the idea of a free personal agent..." "I must write to Mr. Ripley about this matter," he informed a friend in March, 1838.[33]

The idealistic American transcendentalists thus diverged notably from their European socialist contemporaries, the German left Hegelians such as Karl Marx, Moses Hess, and Friedrich Engels. The American transcendentalists were as much socialists as the German group, but the Americans rejected materialism. George Ripley read Ludwig Feuerbach's materialist writings, and rejected them, saying in 1852 that Feuerbach was "crabbed and dogmatic in his atheism"; Marx and Engels, on the other hand, extolled Feuerbach as their materialist mentor. The American transcendentalists based their socialism on a Spinozist pantheism; Marx and Engels turned instead toward a materialist conception of history.[35]

In pre-Civil War America, numerous audiences in Eastern cities and frontier towns learned of Spinoza's import from Ralph Waldo Emerson. That greatest of American teachers, riding indefatigably in the railway cars and stagecoaches along the trail of the lecture lyceums to far-flung points, drew in his famous lecture, "The Over-Soul," the contrast between two types of philosophers, those like "Spinoza, Kant and Coleridge," and on the other hand, those like Locke,

Paley, and Stewart; the "one class speak from *within*, ... and the other class from without, as spectators merely, ..."[36] As far as Emerson was concerned, the latter were of "no use" to him; only those spoke to him who were "parties and possessors of the fact," who felt "that the Highest dwells with him," who felt the "influx of the Divine mind into our mind," experiencing "that Unity, that Over-Soul, within which every man's particular being is contained and made one with all other ...." This was indeed the pantheistic creed that de Tocqueville thought so congenial to democratic nations. But as the smoke of the Civil War battlefields and the ideological fervor receded, even transcendentalists began to feel a certain hollowness in their creed, and to perceive that the harsh reality of sin and suffering were glossed over in the Over-Soul.

IV

The transcendentalists found themselves dissatisfied, as the Civil War ended, with their pre-Civil War metaphysics. Before the war, enthusiastic with Spinoza's concept of an all-inclusive God, they had heard critics charge that Spinoza's views made the fact of Evil as well as man's free choice unintelligible; such objections seemed trivial and puny against their mystical conviction. But not so after the war. It was as if the transcendentalists went through their own "end of ideology," for this phenomenon in the history of ideas was not unlike that which took place after the Second World War when intellectuals of the thirties who had been ardent Marxist determinists decided in the latter forties that an existentialist recovery of the individual's free choice was in order. The war was almost an occasion for the oscillation of the metaphysical wave.

Thus, when the transcendentalists assembled during the post-Civil War years in their Boston Radical Club to hear one of their founders, Frederic H. Hedge, discourse on pantheism, they heard him say: "Spinoza not only denies freedom of will to man, but denies to man substantial existence. He considers the human mind to be part of the infinite intellect of God; . . . In other words, there *is* no such entity as the human mind or soul; . . . " Moreover, since "Spinoza's ontology supposes a single and whole substance, comprising all that is, . . . he is said to have turned the Devil out of the world. There is no room for his Satanic Majesty in a universe which is an expression of God." Consequently: "The great weakness of Pantheism, as expressed by Spinoza, consists in the relaxation of the moral sense consequent on referring all action, good or bad, to God as the one immediate and direct cause of all." Hedge acknowledged "the quickening sense" that Spinoza's philosophy had previously given of "the all-pervading" presence of God, thereby revivifying "a cold and unmeaning dogma."[37] But the distinction of good and evil, in his judgment, likewise vanished if all events were necessitated in God or Nature. The later historian of the movement, Octavious Roy Frothingham, while replying that "Americans are more pantheistic than other peoples because their sympathies are more general and quicker," still felt likewise that "the antithesis between good and evil remained essential to all mankind."[38] The poet Henry Wadsworth Longfellow reminisced that one of his professors had justly warned him and his fellow students many years earlier that Pantheism was "more dangerous" than Atheism "for it rakes away the sense of moral responsibility." The famed Abolitionist militant, Wendell Phillips, veteran of a hundred platforms, added: "Spinoza gives no theory which explains away the fact of suffering, and he had seen suffering which he felt sure was unmitigated evil."[39] In short, it seemed now that life could not be earnest on a Spinozist foundation. One might still admire the character of Spinoza, as Thomas Wentworth Higginson did, for his determination not "to forego his appointed work" even if he had to live "on five cents a day."[40] But even the abolitionist colonel, and the discoverer of the belle of Amherst, the poet Emily Dickinson, seemed to have left aside the Over-Soul. Precisely at this juncture a new variation of Spinoza's thought was developed by the emancipated spirit of Oliver Wendell Holmes, Jr.

The young Oliver Wendell Holmes, Jr. joined the Union Army in 1861 at the age of twenty. At the age of twenty-three, thrice wounded, and mustered out in 1864, his outlook on man and the universe had been recast on the battlefields. He had entered the war as an adherent of the abolitionist ideology ("in the emotional state not unlike that of the abolitionists in former days, which then I shared and now much dislike — as it catches postulates like the influenza," he wrote in 1918). When he emerged, he had henceforth had his "belly full of isms." As a wounded Lieutenant, he had begun to mistrust the facile moralizings of the militant reformers.[41] As a Captain, wounded in the heel, Holmes had prayed that he might lose his foot so that he might not have to return to duty at the front for a third time.[42] During his convalescences he read Lewes' *Biographical History of Philosophy* and above all Spencer's *First Principles* with its conception of an evolving world governed by an all-encompassing law.[43] Good and evil were tested in the crucible of a soldier's experience; the transcendentalist moral absolutes seemed a feeble fortification in the carnage of confusion, cowardice, and courage at Ball's Bluff: "I doubt if the intellect accepts or recognizes that classification of good and bad," wrote the wounded youth.[44] He tried to make his notion of "good" into a synonym for the "general law" of the universe. Recovering from the dysentery after the battle of Fredericksburg, he doubted whether the Union's arms could overcome "the unity or determination of the South," feeling that "civilization and progress" would conquer better in peace than in war.[45]

Probably it was in 1883 that Holmes may have first studied Spinoza's philosophy through the agency of the book by his friend Frederick Pollack, *Spinoza: His Life and Philosophy,* the most influential work in drawing the attention of scholars and philosophers to Spinoza's thought.[46] More than 40 years later in 1927, Pollock wrote Holmes: "You are I think the kind of reader B. d. S. desired. He says expressly that it is not a wise man's part to found a school to be called after his name; and there is nothing to show that he regarded his own work, as final or even finished...."[47] Holmes indeed valued Spinoza precisely because he regarded human good and evil as strictly human responses with no bearing on the meaning of the cosmos as a whole. The transcendentalists had derived from Spinoza an idealistic pantheism in which all living beings shared in the divinity. Holmes washed all such concepts including "natural right" in what he called "cynical acid";[48] the residue that was left of irreducible reality was the notion of contending psychophysical entities, of men, pursuing their fighting faiths, ignorant of any cosmic scheme that underwrote any of them. Spinoza's naturalism was a philosophy congenial to the unsentimental philosophical pharmacologist.

Holmes read and re-read Spinoza's *Ethics.* "If you leave out his logic chopping and theological machinery," he wrote his young friend Harold Laski in 1923, "his view of the cosmos seems to me better than any other I know in the past."[49] With the Sacco-Vanzetti case straining the American legal system, Holmes stated tersely his attitude to systems of philosophy: "All that any of the philosophers has to contribute is a small number of insights that could be told in two minutes ... In 50 years, more or less, the system goes to pot; posterity doesn't care for it — but you have to read the book to get the author's aperçus — ... I care more for Spinoza's than for the other old ones, but I don't believe his postulates or yield to his logic. What I care for is an attitude and a few truths that are independent of his machinery."[50] Holmes saw a world of competing men, classes, nations, and races, struggling against the background of a planet's dwindling resources; civilization resolved itself into a fortunate enclave of "polite manners." It was Spinoza's world divested, however, of God and *amor intellectualis dei*.

The echo, however, of Spinoza's phrases on behalf of freedom of speech can be heard in at least one of Holmes's classical dissenting opinions. In the year 1925, the United States Supreme Court considered the appeal of a New York Communist, Benjamin Gitlow, who had been convicted of "criminal anarchy"; Gitlow had circulated two publications advocating that a dictatorship of the proletariat be established. Holmes had been reading two years earlier "Santayana's charming introduction" to the Everyman's Library edition of Spinoza's *Ethics* that cited the basic proposition of Spinoza's liberalism: "If acts only could be made the ground of criminal prosecutions, and words were always allowed to pass free, sedition would be divested of every semblance of justification, and would be separated from mere controversies by a hard and fast line."[51] This was the doctrine indeed that Holmes was formulating: that freedom of thought reached a limit only when it posed a "clear and present danger." Thus Holmes argued in Gitlow's case that "there was no present danger of an attempt to overthrow the government by force on the part of the admittedly small minority who shared the defendant's views."[52] No doubt the Spinozist influence on Holmes was largely unconscious, dating from his reading of Pollock. "Spinoza has had no conscious influence upon me," he once wrote, though he added, "when I find myself sympathizing with him, the probability of an influence, even if indirect, is great."[53]

The old Civil War veteran in the last 25 years of his life found his chief intellectual joy in the companionship of young Jewish intellectuals. He wondered at this phenomenon himself: "When I think how many of the younger men that have warmed my heart have been Jews I cannot but suspect it," [that "loveableness is a characteristic of the better class of Jews"], wrote Holmes to Laski in 1921.[54] Holmes also told that he had heard say that his ancestors, the Wendells, were Dutch Jews, who had been originally Vondells.[55] Doubtful though this hypothesis of Jewish descent may be, there can be little doubt that Holmes was the most distinguished American thinker to draw sustenance from Spinoza; he imbibed not a theory of God but rather of Nature, the *Natura*, not the *Deus*, the vision of creatures and objects functioning, and man pursuing "an unknown end."[56]

VI

Unquestionably the group to whom Spinoza appealed most were the young Jewish intellectuals, children of the first generation of immigrants to America. Rebels against Jewish orthodoxy, they felt poignantly the division that grew between them and their elders. The young student of philosophy, Morris R. Cohen, twenty-one years of age, wrote that the deepest tragedy in New York's East Side was its conflict of generations affecting the youth with cynicism and pessimism.[57] To these young rebels searching for a masterthinker, the figure of Spinoza, the courageous rationalistic philosopher whom the Jews excommunicated, was a dramatic model.[58] Spinoza seemed to have coped with and solved their own problems; he had united Science and God, combining the deterministic causal laws they learned at college with an infinite God who was Nature; even in studying one's textbook of physics one was engaged in the worship of God, and achieving an intellectual love of Him. Each laboratory experiment became a prayer to God for knowledge of His essence. Cohen in later years thought there was a duplicity in this solution to the generational conflict between science and religion. On the East Side, "to mask our unorthodox ideas," the rebellious intellectuals would "use the word 'God' with Spinoza, to mean what scientists call the system of nature,... Every impulse of filial piety... drove us to this hypocrisy, he said."[59] Yet at the height of his own intellectual powers, Cohen saw no such duplicity, and found a resolving power in "the intellectual love of God." He declared in an essay in 1922: "I undertook to defend the validity of the Spinozistic ideal." For: "Of all philosophers, it seemed to me that Spinoza had most clearly developed the rational and tolerant attitude to the values of religion for which I had been searching." Spinoza left the most "deeply religious" impress, if religion signified "a sense of infinite powers beyond our scope," combined with "a sense of the mystic potency in our fellow human beings." Spinoza, he wrote, "showed me the path to that serenity which follows a view of life fixed on those things that go on," which is imbued with "a sense of the limitations of all that is merely material."[60] From Spinoza, Cohen derived a sense of existence with its unknown infinite attributes, not unlike the Unknowable of Herbert Spencer. At the same time, Spinoza's conviction of the eternity of the human mind was lacking in Cohen's thought; the fact of death for Cohen could not be philosophically overcome as it was for Spinoza: "I cannot agree with Spinoza that the free man thinks of nothing less than of death"; rather the thought of death "is ever present in my mind."

The first Jewish generation to confront death without the sustenance of a religious faith in immortality was all the more drawn to the personality of the excommunicate Spinoza. Perhaps it was a masochistic, self-immolating declaration of loyalty to truth even if it should slay one. But it was peculiarly true that insofar as Spinoza's philosophic reputation was concerned, the fact that he had been excommunicated was the most fortunate thing that could have happened to him. The unconscious of the young Jewish rebels had its own *a priori*: because Spinoza was excommunicated, what he said must be true. Newspaper articles, essays in the *Jewish Daily Forward*, and in such magazines as *The Jewish Tribune*, periodically recounted the exciting tale of the rupture between Spinoza and the Amsterdam Jewish community. The play *Uriel Acosta* was a perennial favorite of the young Jewish intellectuals of the East Side; portraying sympathetically the ill-fated precursor of Spinoza, his bitter battle with Jewish orthodoxy and his final self-destruction, its last act depicted the crushed Acosta transmitting his freethinker's mantle to the child Spinoza.[61]

English agnostics of the nineteenth century had been similarly moved by the character of the excommunicate Spinoza. George Henry Lewes, the life-long companion of the novelist George Eliot, and the author of an influential *Biographical History of Philosophy*, narrated that when he was just over twenty years of age, he hungered for "some knowledge of this theological pariah, partly, no doubt, because he was an outcast, for as I was then suffering the social persecution which embitters all departure from accepted creeds, I had a rebellious sympathy with all outcasts, and partly because I had casually met with a passage, quoted for reprobation, in which Spinoza maintained the subjective nature of evil,..."[62] Lewes encouraged George Eliot in her translation of Spinoza's *Ethics*. Francis Bacon once wrote of the sources of human error — The Idols of the Tribe, the Idols of the Marketplace, the Idols of the Cave, and the Theatre; in strict logic, we might add the Idols of the Pariah, the attraction of the rebellious, the "underdog," the defiant, the truth of the defeated: not "Magna est veritas et prevalebit," but "Magna est veritas et perdet."

Many a young East Side Jew shared in an emotional identification with Spinoza. When Will Durant, later the celebrated author of *The Story of Philosophy*, began his career in 1913 as a popular lecturer at the Labor Temple on Second Avenue and Fourteenth Street, his opening lecture on Spinoza drew "some five hundred new Americans."[63] A Jewish auditor of Durant's versified in a "little magazine":

ON A TALK ON SPINOZA

Durant spoke of Spinoza yesterday
And I sat list'ning, feeling, meditating,
And now and ever afterwards will feel
And live and think more deeply than before,
For having heard Durant speak of Spinoza.

Spinoza! what a mighty, mighty name!
All Alexanders, Caesars and Napoleons —
Mere specks of dust upon a polished lens,
Compared to this poor polisher of lenses.
He polished lenses for myopic eyes; ...

The World's myopic eyes have need of them —
And long will need them — poor myopic world.

My own sight seems improved since I heard
Durant speak of Spinoza yesterday.[64]

Durant's lecture transcribed into a booklet, sold widely as one of the most influential series of cultural publications in American history, the famous Haldeman-Julius Blue Books, retailed at five cents a copy; later it provided the most moving chapter in the still unsurpassed and oft reprinted bestseller *The Story of Philosophy*.[65]

The first American to write a doctoral thesis on Spinoza, Gabriel R. Mason, was indeed one of the young East Side Jews who was in rebellion against the orthodoxy of his parents. Gabriel, himself born in Russia in 1884, was brought by his parents to the United States at the age of eight in

1893. During the year after his Bar-Mitzvah, as he was shedding "the ritual and the superstitions of the Jewish religion," he sought for some sort of intellectual support, or more accurately the reassurance of a tradition within Jewish history of his philosophical rebellion against orthodoxy. To his delight, he came in his senior year at college upon Spinoza, learning that "for these same views Spinoza was excommunicated by the Jews of the Amsterdam Synagogue." Thus, he writes, "I was attracted to this road [Naturalism] by the lovable personality and profound philosophy of Spinoza, . . ."[66] Mason had a notable career as an educator, serving for many years as a principal of a public elementary school and high school, when such posts were the highest academic places to which Jewish scholars, except for unusual exceptions, could aspire. But Mason also was for 44 years a member of the Socialist Party during periods especially before and during the First World War when such a membership brought one close to the permissible boundaries of academic freedom. And if Spinoza lived close to the Collegiant sect, Mason found fellowship in the Ethical Society.

Horace M. Kallen on the other hand, held fast to his ties with the Jewish community, striving rather to re-shape its philosophy to a "Hebraism" that was much influenced by Spinoza. Born in 1883, Kallen was among the very first of the Jewish sons to find in Spinoza a guide-post for liberation. Horace's father, after serving as a Rabbi in Prussian Silesia, had migrated to Boston, Massachusetts; Horace was five years old at the time.[67] Great strains arose between the Rabbinical father and the freethinking son. As Kallen described it in retrospect: "the internal devaluation of Jewish heritage was continuous and progressive. My father was a strict man; I didn't like him; . . ."[68] In later years, Kallen would still recall with some acerbity how his father would humiliate him publicly before his pupils. Horace felt adrift, without intellectual moorings. Then, by chance or divine incursion, as Kallen narrates:

> One day I chanced upon a German rendering of Spinoza's *Theological-Political Tractate*. It set me free. I began to read English versions of his works and English commentaries on these. It was in the year of my graduation from high school that I became enamored of the man and convinced of his philosophy. His image, his thought, and his story became the point of no return in the ongoing alienation from my father and the ancestral religion. I identified with Spinoza.[69]

For a brief period Kallen seems to have shared Spinoza's estrangement from Judiasm. As a Harvard undergraduate, however, he was blessed by the friendship of two great teachers, Barrett Wendell and William James. From Wendell, "a Tory Yankee with Puritan heritage," Kallen acquired a heightened sense of the significance of his Hebraic heritage, while James attracted him toward pragmatism and "radical empiricism." Upon this metaphysics of plural individual realities Kallen based his unique contribution to American thought, the notion of a "cultural pluralism" as America's democratic alternative to the diversity-annihilating concept of the melting pot. Kallen described himself as a libertarian who had been a determinist, a temporalist who had been an eternalist, ... a pluralist who had been a monist, ... The sum of it — a Spinozist who became a pragmatist."[70] Yet if Kallen came to reject Spinoza's determinism, eternalism, and monism, his vision of existence, as set forth in his remarkable *The Book of Job as a Greek Tragedy*, a neglected classic, was embedded in a Spinozist matrix. An impersonal natural order, whose processes and objects forever in flux provide the setting in which man affirms his own unique excellence, was delineated by Kallen: "God is immanent in the movement of events: each is an aspect of him, each reveals him, yet he transcends each and all such ... God is the dynamic of the universe, and the range of his power is co-extensive with it ... In human terms he cannot be thought; being omnipotent, he is self-sufficient, absolute, consequently altogether incommensurable with human nature, ... From any point of view that is human that you may choose, God has no preferences nor can his will and interests be defined in terms of preference."[71] The God that Job finally envisaged, the Infinite Existence of substance and it modes transcending all human standards of good and evil, was for Kallen identical with the "God or Nature" of Spinoza. Although as a Jamesean empiricist, Kallen abandoned altogether the rationalistic theory of knowledge and the pretense of geometrical demonstration from unchallengeable axioms and postulates, the naturalism of Spinoza was retained as a basic tenet.

In Kallen's view, however, Spinoza's "inevitably necessary world of mathematical physics was replaced by the new one of freedom and contingency of physical mathematics." Still, as he estimated Spinoza's significance in 1932 on the three hundredth anniversary of his birth, he declared that though Spinoza's determinism was superseded, "His ethic remains as appropriate to modern conditions of life as it was to his own personal life; nay, far more appropriate."[72]

A striking division of opinion thus characterized the spiritual descendants of Spinoza as to the value of his determinist tenet. Einstein, most notably, quite unlike Kallen, felt that the deterministic tenet was essential for retaining one's sanity in a world consumed by the passions of unreason. "The spiritual situation with which Spinoza had to cope peculiarly resembles our own," wrote Einstein. "The reason for this is that he was utterly convinced of the causal dependence of all phenomena ... In the study of this relationship he saw a remedy for fear, hate and bitterness, the only remedy to which a genuinely spiritual man can have recourse."[73]

Cohen and Kallen, both selective Spinozists, likewise selected and discarded in different ways from their philosophic source. Cohen, as a youthful Marxist and an adherent of the Socialist Labor Party, had valued Spinoza the cosmopolitan who altogether rejected Judiasm, and was indifferent to its continued communal existence. Zionism, Cohen later maintained in a provocative article, was a species of tribalism, and as such, incompatible with the liberal standpoint. To this Kallen replied in his most powerful controversial essay: no, the foundation of Zionism was rather the liberal conviction that "all nationalities are created equal and endowed with certain inalienable rights"; as such, it was continuous with the philosophy of Jefferson's Declaration of Independence.[74] The Jews, as a historic people, "neither better nor worse" than others, are entitled equally to an autonomous existence. Only an abstract internationalism, bred on a theory that levelled all men into "economic men" would obliterate their cultural qualities. Liberalism should rejoice in the cultural diversities of men. Kallen's Hebraism attached a greater significance to the cultures achieved in the temporal flux than did Spinoza for whom the "free man" was essentially a member of a trans-national community of scientists and scholars.

During the post-World War I years until the advent of Hitler, it was the kind of Spinozism that Morris Cohen advocated rather than Kallen's which attracted Jewish college students. During that age of scientism, universalism, and assimilationism, the Menorah Society, for instance, dedicated as it was to Jewish culture, declined in numbers at the City College of New York. Few Jewish students took Zionism seriously, and the feeling was that as liberal democracy took hold, Eastern European Jews as well would find Zionism an obsolete regressive nationalism. Spinoza became the prophet of science and liberalism; the knowledge of science was the knowledge of God. They could regard themselves as disciples of Einstein, the world's greatest Jew, whose "cosmic religion" was the modern equivalent of Spinoza's "intellectual love of God."

Spinoza, indeed, was more often cited in the nineteen twenties as a source of inspiration for Americans than he has ever been since. Indeed, both in political philosophy and metaphysics his name now rarely occurs. His rationalism is out of fashion, and likewise, his freedom from ideology and subservience to the adoration of the masses. His appeal was principally to the second generation young Jews in transition from religion to science. To that generation Morris Cohen and Walter Lippmann were proponents of Spinoza's wisdom.[75]

Cohen and Lippmann, both like Kallen nurtured by William James, and writing their first articles in their organ *The New Republic,* admired Spinoza's conception of life rather than his cosmology. Cohen in 1927 wrote of Spinoza as the "prophet of liberalism" who would have spared America the pathetic humiliations of the era of the Prohibition Amendment;[76] Spinoza had indeed warned that "such attempts have never succeeded in their end," that men will "outwit laws framed to regulate things that cannot be effectively forbidden." Walter Lippmann had listened as a student to his professor, George Santayana, gracefully interpreting Spinoza. Lippmann learned from Spinoza a notion of blessedness that he, a humanist, could accept; blessedness was not the reward of virtue, but virtue itself; the aim of life was not the accretion of things but their enjoyment as objects of reflection; "pure science is high religion incarnate." And Lippmann noted that Spinoza was at one with Freud in his view that "an emotion which is a passion ceases to be a passion as soon as we form a clear and distinct idea of it." On such "disinterestedness," dispassionate understanding, Lippmann felt a humanistic culture could be founded.[77] As America's most influential and analytic political writer,

Lippmann brought this insight to bear upon America's problems during five decades of columns, editorials, and books, in which he appraised the time's turmoil of war, depression, and destruction. Lippmann remained exempt, as Santayana noted, from that "form of cowardice peculiarly modern" of "those who feel safe in their ethics and politics if they are swimming with the tide."[78] Spinoza helped keep Lippmann free from historicism, that ideology which endorses the bandwagon with a metaphysics, and looks at all existence *sub specie politiae.*

VII

The name of Spinoza is little invoked in our own time because his political philosophy has no ideological component. Spinoza offers no law of history, no law of progress, no outline of a Utopia to be achieved. There is no sense of directionality in history from the standpoint of Spinoza's philosophy: "I do not believe that we can by meditation discover in this matter anything not yet tried and ascertained, which shall be consistent with experience or practice . . ."[79] He stands with the tradition of wisdom of Ecclesiastes: "There is nothing new under the sun," and dismisses the aspiration of Platonic philosophers to be king: "No men are esteemed less fit to direct public affairs than theorists or philosophers." For political understanding he turns to experienced practioners in statecraft, to "the most ingenious Macciavelli," to Antonio Perez, the former Secretary of State to the King of Spain, to Pieter de la Court, the economist - collaborator of the Grand Pensionary of Holland.[80] Spinoza's "free man" is not an ideologist seeking a political mandate to fulfill some purported historic mission to realize history's aim. That Spinoza should reject the credentials of philosophers as reliable political advisers might seem strange since he is a philosopher himself. But Spinoza, as we know, ridiculed "the speculations of Platonists and Aristotelians," those who "rave with the Greeks," and he rejected the authority of Plato and Aristotle as not having "much weight with me."[81] He thought of himself as a scientist, a follower of the mathematical method, in the tradition of the ancient materialists.

Spinoza's culminating aim was to provide a set of practical proposals for ensuring the stability of a democratic state. His book of 1670 had extolled democracy as the best form of government, and pointed to the glory of Amsterdam, its liberties and prosperity, as confirming that superiority. The year 1672 had brought the Republic's downfall and the murder of de Witt. He could no more write with assurance about democracy than could a Marxist about Communism after Nikita Khrushchev's speech in 1956 had confirmed the crimes of Stalin's era. In the parts of his *Political Treatise* that were completed before he died in 1677, Spinoza gave a series of specific constitutional provisions for assuring the stability of a monarchy or an aristocracy. What was more important to Spinoza than the form of the government was to insure that, whatever its form, free men would be safeguarded in their liberties. To achieve that goal, there was only one way, and that was to ensure the hegemony of the middle class. He had various empirical models that could guide him in his constitutional theorizing; he used the famed Venice as an example of a stable aristocracy, and Aragon as a model of constitutional monarchy before it was subverted by the absolutist Philip II. But where was he to find an empirical model for a stable democracy? The Athenian history was not one he would emulate; the English colonies in America were small and little known. The Swiss cantons in Spinoza's lifetime were wracked by class struggles and religious civil wars; nor would Spinoza have admired the earlier Genevan democracy, that under Calvin's direction had executed the free man, Servetus.[82] Thus Spinoza's chapters on democracy perforce remained unwritten; the first theorist of democracy in the history of political philosophy could not write the book he wanted to write because he could not find the factual foundation he needed. The philosophy of democracy was born in hope overlayed with uncertainty. Spinoza could not base his democratic standpoint on a belief in the virtues of the comman man, the Lincolnian populist tenet; he had too often asserted the irrationality of the masses. Spinoza was evidently searching for such mechanisms of checks and balances as the Lockean authors of the American Constitution contrived as guarantees against populist and executive despotisms alike. But more than a hundred years of colonial democratic political experience were required to enable such thinkers as Jefferson, Franklin, Madison, and Hamilton to formulate their analyses of the conditions for democratic stability.

Together with Madison and Hamilton, Spinoza shared what might be called the principle of cancellation, namely, that in a large democratic body, the selfish aims of opposing groups and persons tend mutually to cancel each other out; thus, the "pressure groups" and lobbies of workingmen, business executives, bankers, consumers, farmers, all presumably arrive at an equilibrium through the mutual veto and correction of their extravagant claims. Therefore, Spinoza could write that in a democracy "it is almost impossible that the majority of a people, especially if it be a large one, should agree in an irrational design."[83] Precisely herein, however, we do have the most difficult problem of modern democracies; the principle cancellation often fails to work; large powerful unions of workingmen can achieve higher wages, large corporations can raise their prices and profits proportionately or more, while the unorganized consumers, middle classes, and poorer workingmen complain of inflation. A cumulative disequilibrium can also be an outcome of democratic process. Probably such questions were central in

Spinoza's mind after 1672; he did not pretend that he had solved them. No ideological democrat, Spinoza would probably have found congenial the judicious evaluation and concerns of Alexis de Tocqueville's *Democracy in America.* For de Tocqueville, a discerning empirical observer of the democratic American society, and mindful of the universal laws of human nature, was concerned with the preservation of liberties, culture, and science.

Despite his eloquent plea for freedom of speech, Spinoza had small regard for the "schismatics" (or ideologists, as we would say today); "schisms," he writes, "do not originate in a love of truth, ... but rather in an inordinate desire for supremacy."[84] To give ballast to the government against the schismatics, he weighted his constitutions toward the gerontocratic side. Whereas Macciavelli was cooly prepared to resort to a periodic terror to restore political equilibrium, Spinoza proposed instead a standing committee of public safety, made up of older, conservative men, "of an age to prefer actual security to things new and perilous," a constitutional device that the Venetian republic in his view had used.[85] Spinoza, though only 44 years old when he died, was above all concerned with obviating seditious and revolutionary violence.

Lastly, Spinoza is the first philosopher who proposes to assure the stability of the state by harnessing to it the energies of men's "avarice," their passion for accumulation. He is not one of those philosophers such as George Berkeley who deplored the rise of the search for commercial and industrial profit-making; Berkeley indeed had perceived the ruin of Great Britain in the rise of its capitalist civilization, and his theme has echoed in our time in R. H. Tawney's tract against *The Acquisitive Society* and its successor pamphlets and books on the alienation of man under bourgeois society.[86] No, Spinoza aims to take the energies of men as he finds them, and to harness them constructively so that they will contribute to the stability of the commonwealth. Societies, he notes, have hitherto decayed because "men in time of peace... become soft and sluggish." To counteract the evolution toward decadence, Spinoza proposes that the state encourage, honor, and look for others to emulate the accumulators of capital. "And therefore the chief point to be studied," writes Spinoza, "is that the rich may be, if not thrifty, yet avaricious. For there is no doubt that, if the passion of avarice which is general and lasting, be encouraged by the desire of glory, most people would set their chief affection upon increasing their property, without disgrace, in order to acquire honors,...."[87]

Thus, it would follow, according to Spinoza, that only a bourgeois democracy would be a stable democracy. The "decay of capitalist civilization" that has been taking place has not been the outcome of the passion for accumulating capital; rather, as the economist Joseph A. Schumpeter held, it is the spread of the anti-capitalist mentality among intellectuals especially that erodes the self-confidence and enterprising vigor of the capitalist society. When the drive to accumulate is disparaged, the psychological basis of the capitalist economy is undermined. And insofar as liberal democracy is founded on a pluralistic, capitalist economy, with economic power dispersed through a multiplicity of enterprises, it too rests on the freedom of men to venture and accumulate their own capital. Stalin's huge concentration of political power into his dictatorship thus followed on his destruction of private ownership on the farms, his obliteration of the relatively prosperous and more efficient farmers, and his termination of the segments of private commercial and industrial enterprise that Lenin had allowed under his New Economic Policy. The political principles of free thought and speech not only came into existence historically with the advent of Dutch and British capitalism; according to Spinoza's standpoint they were causally grounded in it. As Descartes once wrote, he felt freest doing his writing on the docks of Amsterdam where people were too busy making money to bother about what he was about.[88]

It is strange therefore that Spinoza, the political theorist of bourgeois democracy, has been especially the favorite of so many leftist and socialist-minded youth. Perhaps in part this was because Spinoza renounced trade, became a lens-grinder, and made friends with a religious communitarian group, Collegiant-Mennonites. Then too he was the eloquent advocate of freedom of thought and speech. Nonetheless it is altogether likely that Spinoza would have felt that socialist societies were inherently unstable because they failed to base themselves on the actualities of human nature; such societies became tyrannies precisely because to the extent that their social requirements were inconsonant with the passions of men, they were driven to using compensatory mechanisms of coercion.

VIII

The greatest scientists and philosophers among the Jews in modern times have felt an affinity with Spinoza less as the liberal democrat than as the philosopher of nature. Einstein, Samuel Alexander, and Henri Bergson are men who were stirred by Spinoza's ideas. The fact, however, is that Spinoza might well have repudiated their adaptations of his ideas. He might well have rejected Einstein's concept of the simple order of nature as an "inadequate idea," an all-too-human limitation of God's nature to the capacities of human simple-mindedness; he might have taken umbrage with Alexander's notion of the nisus to Deity as a teleological intrusion upon God or Nature, while Bergson's belief in human freedom he would probably have adjudged as sheer illusion. We would nonetheless suggest that perhaps on a profounder level the tenets of these Jewish thinkers may be found continous with Spinoza's essential vision.

Einstein's conception was, we might say, that the laws of Nature are noumenal; he once said that wherever he approached a problem as to the structure of Nature, he asked himself: "How would God have solved it?"[89] The laws of physics, Einstein felt, would reveal an order, a beauty, a grandeur of simplicity in Nature. Now Spinoza, in his revolt against the notion of purpose in God, repudiates the notion of an "order in nature"; "order" he states, is not a conception of reason but of the imagination, and men attribute it to God because they "prefer order to confusion," wishing to believe that God "has disposed things in which they can most easily be imagined." But God, says Spinoza, can actualize things that "far surpass our imagination."[90] Nonetheless, Spinoza the scientist in practice sought for laws that were so simple, elegant, and rational that they would appear to be identical with logical necessities. A disorderly world would not share this logical character. A multiplicity of Humean universes is alien to Spinoza's essential conception, which Einstein seems to me indeed to embody. The Jewish philosopher of science, Emile Meyerson, who has interpreted the theory of relativity as a geometrizing of Nature in which causes and effect are seen as identities in substance has translated Spinoza's conception of God for the workings of scientific theory.

This world of order to Bergson, however, is pre-eminently that of physical objects. Einstein holds to Spinoza's standpoint that the human mind as well is in all its activities completely governed by deterministic laws. Bergson, on the other hand, availed himself of Spinoza's notion of intuition, the direct insight into truths, this highest mode of knowledge, called by Spinoza "intuitive science," which surpasses both the data of perception and rational analysis.[91] Bergson maintains that we intuit directly our own freedom, that is, our unpredictable creativity; the creative freedom of the human being, his segment of the *elan vital*, his role in the making of reality, operates exempt from determinist law.[92] Now Spinoza was aware that human beings feel they are free. To Bergson he would respond: a stone falling to earth might well think (if it could) that it was creating its own act of descent; this feeling of freedom, Spinoza would argue, is illusory.[93] To which we might answer: a stone, if endowed with consciousness, might rather regard the external gravitational forces as compelling it to move contrary to its own wish to continue in its previous state of motion; the stone's experience of determinism would be that of an externally imposed obliteration of alternatives. Human beings, moreover, do have the experience that causal forms, both external and internal, are not always exclusively decisive, that in the margin of indetermination, their own choices intervene.

Spinoza argues that such phenomena of non-waking life as dreams and sleepwalking are grounds for the belief in mental determinism, because in dreams, "without the direciton of the mind, ... we do some things which we should not dare to do when awake"; our feeling of a "free decree," illusory in dreams, is, he argues, likewise illusory in wakefulness. This conclusion scarcely follows; determinism may indeed characterize our dream contents, but our waking decisions can nonetheless have their ingredient of freedom. "[T]here is nothing which men have less power over than the tongue," says Spinoza, but not all our speech consists of slips of the tongue, for which Freud tried to provide a deterministic explanation. Spinoza would leap from such instances to the belief that all human works of art are likewise determined, but this is a deterministic leap of faith, founded, we might assert, on an "inadequate idea."

Of all Jewish philosophers in the twentieth century, Samuel Alexander probably came closest to the spirit of Spinoza's naturalistic pantheism. He took pride, as he said, "in showing his affiliation to such a philosopher as Spinoza, and the more if he is himself a Jew speaking to Jews..."[94] Yet clearly Alexander's central notion was deeply inconsistent with that of Spinoza's. For a teleological drive characterized Alexander's world of Space-Time; its restlessness, the potent source of new emergent levels, sought the fruition of Deity; beyond present levels of existence, the nisus to Deity pressed for a higher level of qualities surpassing those of man, even as man's emergence had constituted a level rising above its predecessors: "God is the infinite world with its nisus towards deity."[95] Spinoza doubtless chafing at the concept of emergence, would probably insist that the "restlessness" of Space-Time was the outcome of deterministic laws that governed all the emergent levels. Are we then to regard the nisus to Deity as a concept irrevocably incompatible with the directionless, timeless nature of Spinoza's God? It is possible that Spinoza's theology might be enriched by Alexander's conception. For if in the course of time, all the infinite ideas conceived in God's intellect are realized, then at any given time, the actual universe has as yet not actualized an infinite number of possibilities. Spinoza wrote that "desire (*conatus*) is the essence of man," and joy "man's passage from a less to a greater perfection."[96] Even so, insofar as the unrealized possibilities of existence are those of a greater perfection than those presently realized, one might say that a nisus to Deity obtains in the current segment of existence insofar as it moves towards a more perfect level of reality. Until the highest forms of the finite modes of mind have been achieved, God's mind continues to require them. The nisus to Deity is then a corollary of the world's incompleteness in time.

Spinoza, whose ideas have been adapted selectively in ways evidently incompatible with his philosophy as a whole, might conceivably have found himself much at home, and his thought evolving, in the company of his successors, Einstein, Bergson, and Alexander.

FOOTNOTES

1. As Sir Frederick Pollock, the greatest English authority on Spinoza, wrote, shortly before his death: "There have been Kantians and Hegelians according to the letter, ...; there are no Spinozists in that sense but many according to the spirit." Cf. "Contemporary Appreciations of Spinoza," *The Spinoza Quarterly*, Vol. II, No. 2, (1932), p. 94.
2. Professor Vance Maxwell of Memorial University of Newfoundland informs me that H. F. Hallet, the author of *Aeternitatis*, was an exception to my generalization.
3. Noah H. Rosenbloom, *Tradition in an Age of Reform: the Religious Philosophy of Samson Raphael Hirsch*, Philadelphia, 1976, p. 14.
4. "Measure, Time and Number are nothing but Modes of Thought or rather of imagination. Therefore it is not to be wondered at that all who have tried to understand the course of Nature by such notions, ... should have so marvelously entangled themselves ... committing even the most absurd absurdities." *The Correspondence of Spinoza*, tr. A. Wolf, London, 1928, pp. 118-119.
5. *The Chief Works of Benedict de Spinoza*, tr. R.H.M. Elwes, London, 1885, Vol. I, pp. 292, 313, 5.
6. Foucher de Careil, *Réfutation inédite de Spinoza par Leibniz*, Paris, 1854, p. lxiv. *The Oldest Biography of Spinoza*, ed. A. Wolf, London, 1927, p. 180.
7. Spinoza, *The Ethics*, Book I. Appendix. Cf., Spinoza, *Selections*, ed. John Wild, New York, 1930, p. 143.
8. Spinoza, *Ethics*, Book V, Prop. XXIII, Scholium, Wild, ed., p. 385.
9. *Ibid.*, Prop. XLI, p. 397.
10. R.H.M. Elwes, tr., *The Chief Works of Spinoza*, Vol. I, p. 293.
11. Spinoza, *Ethics*, Book IV, Appendix, Par. XXV. Also, Book III, The Affects, Def. XLIV. Wild, ed., *op. cit.*, pp. 360, 279.
12. Frederick B. Tolles, *Meeting House and Counting House: The Quaker Merchants of Colonial Philadelphia, 1682-1763*, 1948, reprinted New York, 1963, p. 175.
13. E. Millicent Sowerby, comp. *Catalogue of the Library of Thomas Jefferson*, Vol. II, Washington, D.C., 1953, pp. 16-17. I am grateful to

Mr. Steven H. Hochman, of the Jefferson Biography Project at the University of Virginia for bringing my attention to these items.

14. Adrienne Koch and William Peden, eds., *The Life and Selected Writings of Thomas Jefferson*, New York, 1944, pp. 705-706.
15. R.H.M. Elwes, tr., *The Chief Works of Spinoza*, Vol. I, p. 263.
16. *Ibid.*, p. 264.
17. *Ibid.*, p. 258.
18. *Ibid.*, pp. 261, 262, 264.
19. *Ibid.*, p. 258.
20. *Ibid.*, pp. 292, 313, 5.
21. Carl Becker, *The Declaration of Independence: A Study in the History of Political Ideas*, New York, 1922, pp. 27-30. Gilbert Chinard, *Thomas Jefferson: The Apostle of Americanism*, Boston, 1929, p. 72 Adrienne Koch, *The Philosophy of Thomas Jefferson*, New York, 1943, p. 138.
22. Spinoza, *The Chief Works*, Vol. I, pp. 243-244.
23. *Ibid.*, p. 340.
24. *Ibid.*, pp. 251, 252, 254.
25. Alexis de Tocqueville, *Democracy in America*, tr. Henry Reeve and Francis Bowen, ed. Phillips Bradley, New York, 1954, Vol. II, p. 33.
26. Ralph Waldo Emerson, *Lectures and Biographical Sketches*, Boston, 1895, p. 110.
27. Theodore Parker, "Transcendentalism," in *The World of Matter and the Spirit of Man*, Boston, 1907, reprinted in George F. Whicher, ed., *The Transcendentalist Revolt against Materialism*, Boston, 1949, pp. 70-71, 77-78. The American democracy, wrote Parker, was founded on a "trancendental proposition." He had been credited with having been the progenitor of Lincoln's phrase, "government of the people, by the people, and for the people." Cf. Henry Steele Commager, *Theodore Parker*, Boston, 1936, p. 266.
28. Charles A. Dana, "Brook Farm," in James Harrison Wilson, *The Life of Charles A. Dana*, New York, 1907, p. 521.
29. Lindsay Swift, *Brook Farm: Its Members, Scholars, and Visitors*, 1899, reprinted, New York, 1961, p. 59. Charles Crowe, *George Ripley: Transcendentalist and Utopian Socialist*, Athens, Georgia, 1967, p. 157.
30. Andrews Norton, *A Discourse on the Latest Form of Infidelity, Delivered at the Request of the Association of the Alumni of the Cambridge Theological School* on the 19th of July, 1839, Cambridge, 1839, pp. 9-11.
31. Octavius Brooks Frothingham, *George Ripley*, Boston, 1882, pp. 98-104. Also cf. Paul F. Boller, Jr., *American Transcendentalism 1830-1860: An Intellectual Inquiry*, New York, 1974, p. 14.
32. R. W. Emerson, W. H. Channing, and J. F. Clarke, *Memoirs of Margaret Fuller Ossoli*, Boston, 1874, Vol. I, pp. 127, 351. Frederick Augustus Braun, *Margaret Fuller and Goethe*, New York, 1910, p. 50. Madeleine

B. Stern, *The Life of Margaret Fuller*, New York, 1942, pp. 157, 184, 304.

33. John J. Duffy, ed., *Coleridge's American Disciples: The Selected Correspondence of James Marsh*, Amherst, 1973, pp. 218-219. Lewis S. Feuer, "James Marsh and the Conservative Transcendentalist Philosophy: A Political Interpretation," *The New England Quarterly*, Vol. XXXI (1958), pp. 14, 20-23. Those New Englanders who early had serious misgivings about transcendentalism were critical of Spinoza's philosophy. Channing and Brownson were of this group. Cf. Robert Leet Patterson, *The Philosophy of William Ellery Channing*, New York, 1952, pp. 64, 95. Henry F. Brownson, ed., *The Works of Orestes A. Brownson*, reprinted, New York, 1966, Vol. I, p. 436, Vol. VI, p. 83 ff. Arthur M. Schlesinger, Jr., *Orestes A. Brownson, A Pilgrim's Progress*, Boston, 1939, p. 154 ff.

34. Frothingham, *George Ripley*, p. 229. Charles Crowe, *George Ripley: Transcendentalist and Utopian Socialist*, Athens, Georgia, 1967, p. 249.

35. There were indeed at least two Jews who were members of the Brook Farm colony, most notably the ebullient Marx E. Lazarus and "his handsome sister"; the literary contributions of Lazarus to the transcendentalist movement are described by Charles L. F. Gohdes as having "surpassed" in number and extent, "those of any other writer for the periodical save the editor himself." Cf. John Thomas Codman, *Brook Farm: Historic and Personal Memoirs*, Boston, 1894, p. 270. Clarence L. F. Gohdes, *The Periodicals of American Transcendentalism*, Durham, 1931, pp. 203, 135, 112. Lazarus, however, for all his ardent blend of Associationism, Abolitionism, Utopianism, Mysticism, and Vegetarianism does not seem to have been a student of Spinoza's thought. Marx Edgeworth Lazarus, a bizarre personality, was probably the first Jewish socialist in the history of the United States; in later years, he served as a private in the Confederate Army, and died in obscurity. Cf. Edgar E. MacDonald, ed., *The Education of the Heart: The Correspondence of Rachel Mordecai Lazarus and Maria Edgeworth*, Chapel Hill, 1977, p. 328.

36. Ralph Waldo Emerson, *Essays, First Series*, Rev. ed., Boston, 1883, p. 269.

37. Mrs. John T. Sargeant, ed., *Sketches and Reminiscences of the Radical Club of Chestnut Street, Boston*, Boston, 1880, pp. 155-157.

38. *Ibid.*, p. 159.

39. *Ibid.*, pp. 159-160.

40. Thomas Wentworth Higginson, *Cheerful Yesterdays*, Boston, 1899, p. 360.

41. Mark De Wolfe Howe, *Justice Oliver Wendell Holmes: The Shaping Years, 1841-1870*, Cambridge, Mass., p. 111. *Holmes-Laski Letters: The Correspondence of Mr. Justice Holmes and Harold J. Laski, 1916-1935*, ed. Mark De Wolfe Howe, Cambridge, Mass., 1953, Vol. I, pp. 164, 689.

42. Howe, *Justice Oliver Wendell Holmes*, p. 155.
43. *Ibid.*, pp. 112, 156.
44. *Ibid.*, p. 106.
45. *Ibid.*, p. 138.
46. *Holmes-Pollock Letters: The Correspondence of Mr. Justice Holmes and Sir Frederick Pollock 1874-1932*, ed. Mark De Wolfe Howe, Cambridge, Mass., 1941, Vol. I, p. 21.
47. *Holmes-Pollock Letters*, Vol. II, p. 203.
48. Oliver Wendell Holmes, *Collected Legal Papers*, New York, 1920, p. 174.
49. *Holmes-Laski Letters*, Vol. I, p. 478.
50. *Ibid.*, Vol. II, pp. 971-972. Also, pp. 939, 1132-1133, 1135.
51. George Santayana, "Introduction," *Spinoza's Ethics and De Intellectus Emendatione*, New York, 1910, 1922, p. xii.
52. Gitlow v. New York, 268 U.S. 652 (1925).
53. Harry C. Shriver, ed., *Justice Oliver Wendell Holmes, his Book Notices and Uncollected Letters and Papers*, New York, 1936, p. 159.
54. *Holmes-Laski Letters*, Vol. I, p. 304.
55. Leonora Cohen Rosenfield, *Portrait of a Philosopher: Morris R. Cohen in Life and Letters*, New York, 1962, p. 443. Also cf. Edmund Wilson, *A Piece of My Mind: Reflections at Sixty*, New York, 1956, pp. 97-98. Beryl Harold Levy, "Justice Holmes and the Jews," *Commentary*, Vol. 22 (Dec. 1956), p. 577.
56. Catherine Drinker Bowen, *Yankee from Olympus: Justice Holmes and his Family*, Boston, 1945, p. 416. Oliver Wendell Holmes, *Collected Legal Papers*, Boston, 1945, pp. 305, 315-316. Holmes's animus against humankind generally grew with time even larger than Spinoza's. Once, when the noted historian, Carl Becker, was visiting him, the Justice said: "Becker, do you love the human race?" Becker replied that though his heart was not one "overflowing with human kindness," he wished them well. Whereupon Holmes answered: "I don't, Becker. God damn them all, I say." Cf. Irving Bernstein, "The Conservative Mr. Justice Holmes," *The New England Quarterly*, Vol. XXIII, (1950), pp. 435-436.
57. William Knight, ed., *Memorials of Thomas Davidson: The Wandering Scholar*, Boston, 1907, p. 87. Thomas Davidson, *The Education of the Wage-Earners*, ed. Charles M. Bakewell, Boston, 1904, p. 113.
58. The socialist historian, Max Beer, noted how Spinoza served as a transitional guide for rebellious Jewish youth. Thus, much earlier, Moses Hess, the "communist rabbi" as Engels called him, and the co-worker of Karl Marx, "read the writings of Spinoza, whither Jewish youths were wont to turn when they strayed from parental faith." Max Beer, *Social Struggles and Modern Socialism*, tr. H. J. Stenning, London, 1925, p. 51.
59. Morris Raphael Cohen, *A Dreamer's Journey*, Boston, 1949, p. 99.
60. *Ibid.*, pp. 216-217.

61. Karl Gutzkow, *Uriel Acosta*, ed. S. W. Cutting and A. C. von Noe, New York, 1910, p. 93 ff. Hutchins Hapgood, *The Spirit of the Ghetto: Studies of the Jewish Quarter in New York*, Rev. Ed., New York, 1909, pp. 122, 166. Harry Roskolenko, *The Time That Was Then: The Lower East Side, 1900-1914: An Intimate Chronicle*, New York, 1971, p. 152.
62. The Editor, "Spinoza," *The Fornightly Review*, Vol. 4, April 1, 1866, p. 387, Lawrence and Elizabeth Hanson, *Marian Evans and George Eliot: A Biography*, London, 1952, p. 178.
63. Will and Ariel Durant, *A Dual Autobiography*, New York, 1977, p. 58.
64. *Ibid.*, pp. 57-58.
65. *Ibid.*, pp. 101-103, 95-96. E. Haldeman-Julius, *The First Hundred Million*, New York, 1928, pp. 107, 130-131.
66. Gabriel Richard Mason, *Gabriel Blows His Horn: The Evolution of a Rebel*, Philadelphia, 1972, pp. 13, 14, 15, 23, 149. Mason's theses, "Spinoza's Idea of God" and "Spinoza and Schelling," secured him the master's and doctor's degrees at New York University, *Ibid.*, p. 16.
67. Horace M. Kallen, *What I Believe and Why — Maybe: Essays for the Modern World*, ed. Alfred J. Marrow, New York, 1971, p. 167. Also cf. Sidney Ratner, ed., *Vision and Action: Essays in Honor of Horace M. Kallen on his 70th Birthday*, New Brunswick, 1953, p. vi.
68. *Ibid.*, p. 181.
69. *Ibid.*, p. 168.
70. *Ibid.*, pp. 166, 182, 169. Cf. M. A. De Wolfe Howe, *Barrett Wendell and his Letters*, Boston, 1924, pp. 183, 185, 273. Robert T. Self, *Barrett Wendell*, Boston, 1975, pp. 140-141.
71. Horace M. Kallen, *The Book of Job as a Greek Tragedy*, 1918, Sec. Ed., New York, 1959, pp. 66, 68, 70.
72. Horace M. Kallen, in "Appreciation of Spinoza," *The Spinoza Quarterly, Tercentenary Issue*, Vol. II, No. 2, November, 1932, p. 105.
73. Albert Einstein, "Introduction," in Rudolf Kayser, *Spinoza: Portrait of a Spiritual Hero*, New York, 1946, p. xi.
74. Morris R. Cohen, "Zionism: Tribalism or Liberalism," *The New Republic* Vol. 18, (March 8, 1919), pp. 182-183. Reprinted in Morris R. Cohen, *The Faith of a Liberal*, New York, 1946, pp. 326-333. Horace M. Kallen, "Zionism: Democracy or Prussianism," *The New Republic*, Vol. 18, (April 5, 1919), pp. 311-313. Reprinted in Horace M. Kallen, *Judaism at Bay: Essays toward the Adjustment of Judaism to Modernity*, New York, 1932, 1972, pp. 111-120.
75. During the latter twenties, on December 18, 1927, a society actually was founded in New York City called the Spinoza Institute of America. It organized public lectures on Spinoza at one of which, for instance, at the Stuyvesant High School, Morris R. Cohen was the speaker, and Gabriel R. Mason the chairman. One of its grouplets under the guidance of a Marxist, Harry Waton, tried to synthesize Marx and Spinoza. The

Spinoza society published irregularly for a few years a journal called *The Spinoza Quarterly* that enlisted brief statements from Romain Rolland, Albert Einstein, Sir Frederick Pollock, and several Harvard luminaries. The little sect took on all the traits peculiar to an association of crackpots, with a creed called "biosophy," and its creedal leader; its existence became shadowy as the years of depression ended. Harry Waton continued into the early 50's to give lectures at the Labor Temple under the banner of the Spinoza Institute of America; copies of them were deposited in the Archives of the New York Public Library. Waton, with an original flair, argued that Marx's historical materialism defined the physical order of things which in accordance with Spinoza's psycho-physical parallelism, had to be complemented with the historical idealism of mental realities. Cf., Harry Waton, "Why a Spinoza Institute?", in Spinoza Institute of America, *Baruch Spinoza: Addresses and Messages Delivered and Read at the College of the City of New York on the Tercentary of Spinoza*, November 23, 1932, New York, 1933, pp. 65-77. Harry Waton, *Marxism Reconsidered: Should We Go Beyond Marx?*, Brooklyn, 1940, p. 5.

76. Morris R. Cohen, "Spinoza: Prophet of Liberalism," *The New Republic*, Vol. 50, (March 30, 1927), pp. 164-166; reprinted in *The Faith of a Liberal*, New York, 1946, pp. 13-19.

77. Walter Lippmann, *A Preface to Morals*, New York, 1929, pp. 192, 34, 43, 220-221, 239.

78. George Santayana, "Enduring the Truth," *The Saturday Review of Literature*, Vol. 6, Dec. 7, 1929, p. 512.

79. *The Chief Works of Benedict de Spinoza*, tr. R.H.M. Elwes, Vol. I, *Tractatus Theologicio-Politicus, Tractatus Politicus*, London, 1883, p. 288.

80. *Ibid.*, pp. 287-288, 315, 334, 360.

81. *Correspondence*, p. 290. *The Chief Works of Benedict de Spinoza*, Vol. I.

82. E. Bonjour, H. S. Offler, G. R. Potter, *A Short History of Switzerland*, Oxford, 1952, pp. 193-195.

83. *The Chief Works of Benedict de Spinoza*, Vol. I, p. 206.

84. *Ibid.*, Vol. I, p. 265.

85. *Ibid.*, p. 380.

86. George Berkeley, "An Essay Toward Preventing the Ruin of Great Britain" (1721), in *The Works of George Berkeley*, ed. Alexander Campbell Fraser, Oxford, 1901, Vol. IV, pp. 321-338.

87. *The Chief Works of Benedict de Spinoza*, Vol. I, p. 381.

88. Descartes wrote from Amsterdam on May 5, 1631, to his friend Balzac that in the city of merchants he found perfect solitude and comfort: "en cette ville où je suis, n'y ayant aucun homme, excepté moi, qui n'exerce la marchandise, chacun y est tellement attentif à son profit, que j'y pourrais demeurer toute ma vie sans être jamais vu de personne." The alienation from the cities would have been an incomprehensible

fashion to Descartes. He continues: "The noise of the traffic interrupts my meditations no more than would the flow of the river." He is filled with pleasure "à voir venir des vaisseaux, qui nous apportent abondamment tout ce qui produisent les Indes, et tout ce qu'il y a de rare en Europe." "Can you tell me another country where so complete a liberty can be enjoyed; where one can sleep more quietly; where there are soldiers ready to guard us; where poisoning, treason, and calumnies are less known; and where more of the innocence of our ancestors remains to us?" Spinoza shared the same enthusiasm for the merchants' democracy. Descartes, *Correspondence*, ed. Ch. Adam and G. Milhaud, Paris, 1936, Tome 1, 189-191. Elizabeth S. Haldane, *Descartes: His Life and Times*, London, 1905, pp. 115-116.

89. Lewis S. Feuer, *Einstein and the Generations of Science*, New York, 1974, pp. 78-80. Leopold Infeld, *Quest: The Evolution of a Scientist*, New York, 1941, p. 267. Also cf. Albert Einstein, *The World as I See It*, tr. Alan Harris, New York, 1934, pp. 264-267. Einstein wrote appreciatively of Spinoza's determinism on the occasion of the 300th anniversary of Spinoza's birth: "Spinoza ist der Erste gewesen, der den Gedanken der deterministischen Gebundenheit allen Geschehens wirklich konsequent auf das menschliche Denken, Fuhlen und Handeln angewendet hat. Nach meiner Ansicht hat sich sein Standpunkt unter den um Klarheit und Folgerichtigkeit Kämpfenden nur darum nicht allgemein in durchsetzen konnen, weil hierzu nicht nur Konsequenz des Denkens, sondern auch eine ungewohnliche Lauterkeit, Seelengrosse und — Bescheidenheit gehört." Siegfried Hessing, ed., *Spinoza: Dreihundert Jahre, Ewigkeit, Spinoza Festschrift*, 1632-1932, Den Haag, 1962, p. 196. Also, Albert Einstein, "Tercentenary Message," in Spinoza Institute of America, *Baruch Spinoza* New York, 1933, pp. 28-29.

90. Spinoza, *Ethics*, Book I, Appendix. Wild, ed., op. cit., p. 139.

91. Spinoza, *Ethics*, Book II, Prop. XL., Scholium 3.

92. Henri Bergson, *An Introduction to Metaphysics*, tr. T. E. Hulme, 2nd ed., New York, 1955. Henri Bergson, *Creative Evolution*, tr. Arthur Mitchell, New York, 1911, pp. 238-239. S. Zac, "Les Thèmes Spinozistes dans la Philosophie de Bergson," in *Les Etudes Bergsoniennes*, Vol. VIII, Paris, 1968, pp. 146-147. Cf. Henri Chevalier, *Henri Bergson*, tr. Lilian R. Clare, New York, 1928, p. 320.

93. Spinoza, *Ethics*, Book I, Appendix. Book III, Prop. II, Scholium.

94. Samuel Alexander, *Space and Time*, London, 1921, p. 79. Samuel Alexander, *Space, Time and Deity*, London, 1920, New Impression, 1927, Vol. I, pp. xiii-xv, Vol. II, pp. 45, 345. Also cf. Samuel Alexander, *Philosophical and Literary Pieces*, ed. John Laird, London, 1939, pp. 62, 67, 385.

95. Samuel Alexander, *Space, Time and Deity*. Vol. II, p. 353.

96. Spinoza, *Ethics*, Part III, Proposition LIX, The Affects. Wild, ed., op. cit., p. 266.

SPINOZA ON MAN'S KNOWLEDGE OF GOD:
Intuition, Reason, Revelation, and Love
David Savan[*]

The very center of Spinoza's philosophy is his conception of God and the complete dependence of human well-being upon God. Yet very few of the many academic philosophers who write today about Spinoza focus directly upon this center. It seems to me appropriate, in this College and on this commemorative occasion, that we should think again about Spinoza's intense metaphysical concern with God and our relation to God.

Spinoza was utterly convinced that he had discovered the fountainhead of everything that exists and the foundation of all knoweldge and emotion. "I do not presume that I have found the best philosophy," he wrote to a friend, "but I know that I think the true one."[1] The truth which Spinoza believed he had demonstrated reveals itself in all of nature and in all our experience. Our own bodies and minds, and all things in the universe, exhibit God in the most direct way. "Every idea of every body or individual thing actually existing necessarily involves the eternal and infinite essence of God."[2] "Nothing can be conceived without God."[3] Furthermore, "he who understands himself and his affects clearly and distinctly, loves God, and loves him better the better he understands...."[4]

But then, you may well ask, why do we need a philosopher of genius to discover for us what we all know? And why,

[*]Dr. David Savan is Professor of Philosophy at the University of Toronto.

after it is discovered, is it developed in such technical and difficult argument? The answer is that it is our pressing practical concerns which, unavoidably, obscure our knowledge of God. We imagine God as a father, a king, and a lawgiver because we desperately hope to persuade Him by prayer and sacrifice to grant us what we need and desire. Nevertheless, said Spinoza, within these imaginings and desires there lies a shadowed but true conception of God. Spinoza hoped that, like a chemist, he could purify and clarify this true conception. He hoped that by precise definition he could remove all imaginative accretions, and by mathematically demonstrative deduction he could set out the correct order of dependence.

Spinoza admired Euclid's geometrical method, because it is maximally free from personalities and from the limitations which a particular culture places upon our understanding and communication. However great might be the distance between Euclid's times and his readers', the arguments remain clear and distinct. Spinoza aimed at this same transcultural directness. It is an ironic paradox that it is in part because he adopted the Euclidean method that his own conception has been shadowed and obscured. He did not foresee how soon his own philosophical vocabulary would become nearly incomprehensible. And he was wrong in thinking, as do many philosophers today, that by using mathematical methods philosophy can achieve mathematical clarity and certainty. For this and other reasons I believe than Spinoza's conception of God has often been misunderstood, with serious consequences for the interpretation of his philosophy of human understanding, action, passion, and politics. My intention in this talk is to elucidate Spinoza's certainty that God is most directly revealed to all of us, and yet that God can be adequately understood and loved only through intellectual intuition.

When we live through an earthquake of major proportions we discover in a flash how utterly dependent we are on something we normally don't even think about. We are suddenly utterly helpless. In one of his rare autobiographical passages, in his *Treatise on the Improvement of the Understanding*, Spinoza wrote that he went through such a spiritual earthquake. "I perceived that I was in a state of great peril, and I compelled myself to seek with all my strength for a remedy, however uncertain it might be; as a sick man, struggling with a deadly disease, when he sees that death will surely be upon him unless a remedy is found, is compelled to seek such a remedy with all his strength, inasmuch as his whole hope lies therein."[5]

Spinoza was well aware of the danger that faces those who, like himself, are alive to their desperate need to find God. How can we be sure that we have not ourselves created a fiction, a wish-fulfilling God made in our own image? Spinoza believed that he was protected against this danger. He claimed to know God directly and immediately. His philosophy demonstrates, he believed, not only that he and all human beings have direct knowledge of God but that we must *necessarily* have such knowledge. God is not mediated. We do not need to know Him through miracles, or on the authority of go-betweens, messengers, or prophets. "We cannot be more certain of the existence of anything than of the existence of a being absolutely infinite or perfect, that is, God."[6] We do not infer the existence of God as the conclusion of an argument because He is better known than any possible premises. What Spinoza claimed to demonstrate by his argument is the *necessity* with which God must exist. Those who analyse Spinoza's argumentation sometimes overlook the fact that he wrote in the belief that he and his readers have direct knowledge of the living God.

Nevertheless, God is not a singular individual being, whether finite or infinite, whether natural or beyond nature. We cannot form a picture of God, and it is wrong to form an image of God as masculine or feminine.[7] On the other hand, many medieval philosophers conceived of God as *being as such*. This is to escape Scylla only to flounder on Charybdis. *Being* is a transcendental term, Spinoza argued, both abstract and general. Such terms are in the highest degree confused. They attest to the limitations of the human imagination. God is not general and confused but in the highest degree concrete and clear.

Everything turns on what Spinoza understands God to be. Some have taken Spinoza's famous phrase, *Deus sive Natura*,[8] to indicate the answer. If only Spinoza had not been so concerned to avoid persecution by the orthodox public of his time, so this interpretation runs, he would have written openly that all men know nature as the infinite temporal series of causes and effects, that in knowing ourselves and the things around us we come to know nature more fully, that in so doing we come to love nature, and that in this love of nature we find our blessedness and peace of mind. Such an interpretation is mistaken, and Spinoza would condemn this way of thinking as a new superstition.

When Spinoza spoke of *God or Nature* he must have meant by *nature*, we assume, what we mean by that word. I won't ask whether we do in fact know just what we mean by *nature*, but in Part I of the *Ethics* Spinoza tells us what he means. God is *natura naturans*, active, productive and free nature, and not *natura naturata*, nature passive, enacted, datum. *Natura naturata* is the infinite and enduring universe which is in God, and is the expression of God. But it is not God. So when Spinoza used the phrase *Deus sive Natura* he was saying that God is substance, and stressing that God's essence is free causal activity. "It is as impossible for us to conceive that God does not act as that he does not exist,"[9] he wrote.

If we wish to understand God as Spinoza understood Him we must ask what he meant by *free cause* and by *substance*. It will then be easier to see what sort of activity is essential to God. At this point we cannot avoid the use of some of the technical terminology Spinoza inherited from earlier philosophers. In the opening definitions of the *Ethics* it is clear that a free cause is a self-caused thing (*causa sui*), insofar as it acts. Something is a free cause if its essence entails its existence and action, that is, if its nature cannot be conceived except as existing and acting. In this definition the word "essence" needs explanation. What is meant by *essence?* The essence of a thing is (1) that in the thing which *must* remain the same throughout all the changes the thing may undergo, so long as that thing retains its individual identity, and (2) is at least theoretically definable or capable of being understood and conceived. In brief, the essence of a thing is that which is necessary to the intelligible identity of that thing.

A few illustrations may make this more clear. The essence of an abstract thing like a triangle is that it is a plane figure bounded by three intersecting straight lines. A particular natural thing, triangular in shape, may change in various ways — it may change color or size, for example — but so long as the essence remains true of it we have a triangular thing. What is the essence of a human being? Let me use an example discussed both by Wittgenstein and Kripke — Moses. The specific events in Moses' life might have varied indefinitely and yet he could have remained the same person. Someone other than Pharaoh's daughter might have rescued him. He might not have been the leader who brought us out of slavery in Egypt. The criteria by which his contemporaries identified him — perhaps a stammer, or a distinctive appearance, voice, or gait — might have been otherwise. Still, Spinoza and those who agree with him that there must be something essential to the identity of any individual thing would say that so long as Moses remains Moses his essence must remain. Moses' essence is a specific balance of physical energies, a specific psychological structure, and underlying these a distinctive power of action in relation to God.

Now the essence of any natural thing can, at least in theory, be conceived even if the thing does not exist here and now. I can conceive of a triangle even if there were in fact no existing triangles. I can conceive of Moses even though he no longer exists. As Spinoza put it, "the essence of things produced by God does not involve existence."[10] Such things are usually said to be contingent. But a free cause is different. Its essence cannot be conceived or in any way thought unless it exists. Not only does it exist — it *must* exist. Its essence guarantees its existence, so that if we think it, its existence is immediately present in what we are thinking. Spinoza gave his readers at the very outset a criterion by which to identify what he meant by God. Ask yourself, he implied, whether you have a concept or thought which, by its very nature, guarantees that it is not empty.

I'd like to suggest a philosophical analogy which you may find helpful. Most of the true sentences we utter are true because the facts are as the sentences says they are. The sentence alone does not guarantee its own truth. If I say, "I am happy now," that may be true, but it is not true by virtue of the words but because in fact I *am* happy. There are sentences, however, called *analytic* by philosophers, which do guarantee their own truth, regardless of the empirical facts. "If I am happy, then I am happy." "Either it's raining or it's not raining" — these are analytically true sentences. They guarantee their own truth. Spinoza's free cause might be called, after this analogy, a metaphysically analytic existence. Its meaning guarantees its existence.

Substance is the converse of a free cause. Substance is that whose existence entails its essence. As he put it, substance is that which is in itself and is conceived through itself, i.e. through its own existence. The very definition or nature of substance is to be and, through that very fact, to be conceived. This is Spinoza's second criterion by which we may identify what he means by God. Ask yourself this second question: Is there an existence which is such that of itself, without calling upon anything else, it guarantees that it is conceived?

Let me suggest another analogy, imperfect though it is. Assume that we know only one language — English, let's say — and that all our thinking is in English sentences. Now many of the things that exist are not known by us — distant stars, people in far away places, etc. These things we won't talk about, since we don't know them. And the things that we do know will not be thought or described through themselves but through the language that we all speak. But there will be one existing thing that we do know through itself, and that we talk about and think about through itself — the English language. We have made it an assumption that we speak and understand it. If we say, for example, "'word' and 'English' are English words," or "Every well formed English sentence has a subject and a predicate," these sentences are talking about English through itself, in English. On the other hand, when we talk about anything other than English we talk about that thing through something other than itself, namely through English.

Now, perhaps, we are in a better position to understand what it means to say that nature, understood as *natura natuata,* consists of things and events which we can conceive even when they don't exist, and which, when they do exist, are not conceived through themselves. God, on the other hand, is that whose essence involves his existence, and whose existence of itself insures that He is conceived or known through Himself. We set out to find the answer to the question, what does Spinoza understand God to be? There is only one answer which satisfied our two criteria. God is that whose essence is one and the same as existence.[11] God is existence itself. By existence, recall, Spinoza does not mean general and abstract being. Existence is concrete activity, pulsating, changing, obdurate, positive, filling with its infinite variety every place in this infinite natural universe.

Existence cannot be destroyed or created. It is particular and individual things that come into existence or pass out of existence. But notice that when something ceases to exist it leaves no gap or vacuum in existence. The non-existence of one thing is the existence of something else that replaces it. Even the concrete but empty space of the universe is, on Spinoza's view, an infinite mode of existing. It exists as distance, as quantity measured by motion. Things must endure through time as they move through empty extension. The space of Euclidean geometry (as distinct from the space of the actual universe) is an abstraction because the endurance of existing things is irrelevant to it.

All things are in existence, but existence itself is not in anything other than itself. We cannot conceive of any division or break within it, or of any boundary or limit which could reduce its infinity. We cannot derive the conception of existence from anything prior to or simpler than itself, and if we did not understand it through itself we could never know that anything — including ourselves — exists. We know what it is to exist in our every fibre, and we know it in everything we encounter.

Some years ago W. V. Quine asked the question, what is there? And he gave an answer: everything! True enough, but trivial, empty, uninformative, uninteresting. That, of course, was Quine's point. But, it will be objected, isn't Spinoza's answer to the question, what is God, equally trivial, empty, and uninteresting? Perhaps — so the objector might continue — Spinoza's answer is not false and also not true. Perhaps it is simply meaningless.

Spinoza did not have at his disposal the subtle theory of meaning which has been developed in the last hundred years. Metaphysical concepts and arguments were more readily acceptable to the intellectual community of his time than they are today. Nevertheless, Spinoza was well aware of the attacks to be expected both from skeptics, who denied that knowledge for certain was possible, and from religious dogmatists, who rejected all departures from orthodoxy and suspected all philosophical argumentation. Spinoza's reply to the accusation of triviality was to point to the nontrivial consequences which he drew from his conception of God. I will discuss some of these shortly. His reply to the accusation that his conception of God as concrete active existence is meaningless is to turn the tables and counter-attack. The rejection of his conception of God is "to say that he had a true idea and nevertheless doubted whether or not it was false."[12] The self-contradiction and loss of meaning lies, he contended, on the side of his critics.

Briefly, Spinoza's argument is as follows: we must all know the difference between saying of any particular thing that it exists or that it doesn't exist. Otherwise there would be no sense in saying that a sentence like "Peter exists" is true and not false. Further, existence itself is one and the same whether what exists is Peter, or a star, an electron, an idea, a mind. In philosophical terminology, existence is a univocal term. Even when we think and say what is false, something or other must exist, even if it is only that false sentence or an illusory idea. It is always possible, at least in theory, to attain true knowledge of what that something or other is that does exist in the illusion or error. If existence were meaningless or self-contradictory then the existence of Peter or of any other thing would be meaningless or self-contradictory, and both truth and falsity would be impossible. Nothing outside existence can prevent or limit it, since what is outside existence does not exist. It follows then, according to Spinoza, that there is existence and that it must be conceived independently of any particular thing or of any finite collection of particular things.

Existence is not an idea or concept, although an idea may be in existence. That's why Spinoza says all ideas are in God. Existence isn't a thing (in his terminology, it isn't a mode), but a thing may be in existence. Hence he says that whatever is, is in God.[13] Existence cannot be imagined, and when we try to form an image of it we see it erroneously as some kind of force, separate from its modes, mysterious, unfathomable, propelling a world of passive objects. No, existence can only be conceived. It must be conceived as expression and self-manifestation without limit, as the infinite activity exhibited in all things in infinite ways. We conceive it in the motion and rest of extended things and in the thinking which forms ideas, but there is no limit to the infinite but unimaginable ways in which it is conceivable.

We cannot form any general idea of God. That is to say, we cannot classify or categorize Him so as to conceive of a possible second or third entity of the same kind with which He could be compared. To apply number to anything, even the number one, that thing must first be classified under some general concept, Spinoza wrote.[14] If I hold up my hand

and say, "this is one," that statement is true of the hand, but not true if you think of the five fingers or the numerous cells. Notice, however, that in thinking of this as one hand you are conceiving the theoretical possibility of other things that might also be classed as hands. But we cannot even conceive the theoretical possibility of a second God. We are speaking, remember, of that whose definition or essence is simply active existence. So anything else of the same definition or essence must be identical with it. There cannot be any other existence which could distinguish them in the way that space or time can distinguish two identical twins or two identical electrons. Strictly, then, we cannot apply any number to God, not even the number one. God is not *a* unique thing. He is uniqueness itself.

This is also the reason why Spinoza wrote that God acts necessarily and yet freely.[15] God's action is absolutely free because there is nothing within Him or beyond Him which can limit or compel Him. But God acts necessarily because no alternative is possible or conceivable. It makes no sense to suppose that existence could be or act otherwise than it does.

Spinoza didn't deny that we think about what doesn't exist, about fictions, myths, hypothetical entities, and unrealized possibilities. We make mistakes and think what is false. But in all these cases, he argued, we must first think and know what does exist in order to think about what does not exist. Saul Kripke, the philosopher who laid the foundation for what is called possible world semantics, recently pointed out — in a quite Spinozistic spirit — that when we speak of possible worlds we don't find them by looking through an intellectual telescope. A possible world is a way of supposing that what does in fact exist may be varied, contrary to fact. So we start always from where we are, from what does exist, from what some philosophers call *indexicals*.

It was Spinoza's position that underlying every possibility, and within every falsehood there is some existent truth which it is the task of science to lay bare. Suppose I think of a candle burning in a vacuum. Here I am not deceived because I know that I have seen an actual candle burning and I have simply abstracted from it the air and other circumstances which make the burning possible. Suppose next that I am actually deceived by some optical illusion — Spinoza's example was the sun reflected in the water. Someone might be deceived into thinking that a bright disc is under the water. I am deceived, perhaps, because I don't know the laws of optics, or the principles of vision, or perhaps I am ignorant of some other actual facts. But, if, in this and all other cases of error, I come to know the existing causes and how they operate to produce my error, then there is no longer any falsehood. In fact, I may come to recognize that the error was inevitable and necessary, and this knowledge of the necessity of error is itself testimony to the power of science and the strength of the human mind. Notice that when we understand its causes, the illusion doesn't disappear. The bright disc continues to look as if it were in the water. Only the power to deceive is gone. "Just as light reveals both itself and the darkness, so truth is the standard of itself and of falsehood."[16]

Spinoza went further. Once we understand the existent causes of the optical illusion we can see that the power of the imagination is a virtue of the mind and not a defect.

We can now understand that the illusion reveals the intrinsic and free power of the eye, light, etc.[17] Here we begin to see what Spinoza meant by revelation. Revelation is sure knowledge revealed by God to man, and shining forth from within our imagination. Like the light which reveals itself and darkness, God reveals himself in the midst of our history, our struggles, our victories, and our defeats.

Now, I hope, we are closer to understanding what Spinoza understood God or *natura naturans* to be. God is the activity of expressing the absolute, affirmative, and eternal uniqueness of existence itself, through the infinite variety of finite natural things. Each finite thing expresses, in its own unique individuality, the unique activity of God. The necessity of God's activity is expressed in the fact that it is inconceivable, if Spinoza is right, that any particular thing should be or act otherwise than it does. The freedom of God is expressed in the fact that each natural thing acts out its own nature freely but within the limits which its environment allows. This combination of necessity and freedom means that God's activity is the infinite differentiation and variation of nature. Some writers on Spinoza have accused him of denying individuality. I am amazed. If I understand him correctly, he is the philosopher of individuality *par excellence*. He is saying not just that no two things are exactly alike, but that it is inconceivable that they should be exactly alike or act in exactly the same ways.

There is an obvious objection which should be considered. The answer may help clarify Spinoza's position. The objection is simple enough. There are many counter-examples to Spinoza's thesis. Something may be unique, like a novel, but this doesn't hinder the press from running off thousands of identical copies. Something may be unique and without copies, like a building, but it may consist of many identical parts — arrays of columns, for example, or many carefully measured stones. Similarly, why shouldn't God be unique while two or more things in *natura naturata* are identical and interchangeable?

This objection misses Spinoza's point, because he intends to deny any analogy between God and a natural object. God is not a thing, but unlimited expressive activity. He cannot be imagined but only conceived. And He cannot be conceived through analogy with anything; He must be conceived through Himself. Each distinct finite thing is a node within an infinite network which expresses the unlimited activity of God. There is no conceivable standard by which to measure alternative possibilities except what does in fact exist. The very idea itself of alternative possibilities is an existing idea, a mode of thought, and cannot be conceived to be other than it is. If two distinct things exist, then no matter how much like one another they may otherwise be, it is just that minimal distinction that is their being two and not one that is necessary and without alternative.

It follows that existence is double. In itself, as God, it is a unique generative activity, expressing and dividing itself infinitely. As *natura naturata* it is infinitely multiplied, diversified, particularized. Different as they are, active nature and passive nature cannot be separated. It is of the essence of God that He expresses Himself without limit. It is of the essence of the world that it is in God and is conceived through Him. In all our experience we know both activity and passivity at once and together. Only abstractly, in words, can the two aspects to be held apart.

The last four parts of the *Ethics* carry through the implications of this conception of God. I would like to sketch some of these consequences in the rest of this talk. Every single thing is a distinctive and irreplaceable power of acting. It is this power of acting that Spinoza called the *essence* of the thing. The activity of each finite thing is limited by the activities of the rest of nature. Different things are distinguished from one another by the degree of their activity in competition with the activities of the rest of nature. Ultimately, each thing will perish. Nevertheless, even the most fragile of things — a rainbow, a dream, or a puff of smoke — acts so long as it exists, and its activity is positive, affirmative. This essential self-affirmation, when it is considered as opposed to the action of external things upon it, Spinoza called *conatus* — the endeavor of a thing to persevere in its own activity. It is not a striving toward any goal, and it is not measured by the length of time a thing endures. That, after all is subject to accident. A human being might live for only a few minutes while a puff of smoke might survive for hours if circumstances were propitious. *Conatus* is simply the positive and distinctive activity of a thing.

What is true of all natural things is true also of man. But the human body is a higher degree of activity than the other physical things around it because the human body is able to maintain its identity through a greater variety and a greater amplitude of interactions with its environment than other bodies. The first thing that constitutes the human mind, according to Spinoza, is the idea of that body. This idea is at first more a vague, tangled, semi-conscious feeling than a distinct thought. Spinoza called this ground feeling of our own positive identity our primary affect or emotion. It is not a primal scream but a primal joy, the sensation of our fundamental self-affirmation. It is our answer, *Hineini*, "Here am I," to God's call.

In his earliest work, the *Short Treatise*, Spinoza seems to have identified this primal feeling with the most elementary form of love, "to enjoy a thing and be united with it," as we enjoy our own existence and are united with it. In his *Ethics* Spinoza changed his terminology and called this primary feeling *desire*. But this primary libido, desiring love or loving desire, is already in a confused way a love of God because it is a love of a unique existent. Pain and sorrow are the feeling of our own weakness before the power of other things. We hate or fear what we imagine weakens us. But when we imagine that something increases our power we feel joy and delight, and we love whatever gives us this heightened joyful vitality. Of course, it is human beings who can most fully help us and sustain us, and it is human beings whom we love — at first ourselves, then our mother, our father and outward in an expanding circle. In one letter Spinoza suggested that a father and son may be so closely identified as to share the same images and feelings.[18] The primary kinship which we feel with any human being, simply because we imagine that he or she shares our own unique identity brings with it a basic human sympathy, a fellow-feeling. So love is prior to hate. When I imagine that another person diminishes me I hate him or her, and I express this hate by imagining that person as no longer human, as a pig, or dog, or — so Spinoza interpreted the story of the Garden of Eden — a snake.[19] Nevertheless, so long as I see another person as human I feel for him or her a sympathy which is prior to any hatred I may come to feel.

Love at this basic level of unthinking feeling is then, on Spinoza's view, simply the expansion to include other human beings of my feeling of my own distinctive power. Within this love, without at first clearly and distinctly understanding it, I love God. This is the truth which is revealed in the life of a person and also in the history of a people. Thus God reveals himself to us. "From the Bible itself," Spinoza wrote, "we learn, without the smallest difficulty or ambiguity, that its cardinal precept is: To love God above all things, and to love one's neighbor as oneself."[20] It was not Spinoza's view that the Scripture teaches only laws, which the unenlightened must be induced to obey. Through the histories and the human imagination it reveals that God's truth is love. Spinoza confessed that he did not understand how it came about that this or that prophet came to see this truth. But he shared the certainty of it with the prophets.

Because revelation is in time and history, it does not show us causes and reasons. It is a light which shines in the midst of darkness. Reason, on the other hand, does give us clear and distinct understanding of the similarities and differences which relate all things to one another. Reason — deductive thinking — sees what Spinoza called the *infinite modes,* those laws of motion and rest which run through the whole universe and are equally in the parts and in the whole. Therefore, he wrote, reason cannot be, nor can it show us, the essence of any individual thing.[21] It can show us necessary connections and disjunctions, but it cannot tell us what exists, what is the case. It gives us laws, but laws without love. Applied to human society, reason shows us how society is best organized, how the state serves human needs, how to act rationally. But all this without feeling and without love.

Spinoza did not condemn or abjure reason. Quite the contrary. It is essential for the correction of error, for the control of the passions, for law and regularity in human association. Still, if men were purely rational and nothing else, they would form no conception of evil — but also no conception of good. They could not, in that event, pursue their own good, their own self-affirmation. Although passion without reason is blind, reason completely devoid of passion is empty. Reason must be applied to the control of the passions in the same way that it is applied to the improvement of our sight, hearing, or locomotion. When we understand our passions rationally we do not eliminate them, any more than we eliminate illusions when we understand their causes. It is impossible that man should not be part of nature.[22] "An affect (i.e. emotion) cannot be restrained or removed except by an opposed and stronger affect."[23] Reason can control and regulate the passions, but only by using one passion against another. Still, there is joy in this power we have through reason to control the passions. It is an increase in our power of acting and therefore is felt as joy.

I have been emphasizing this aspect of reason not only because it is frequently overlooked or misunderstood, but because I want to show the significance of *scientia intuitiva*, and why it, and not reason, is essentially connected with the intellectual love of God and with our eternity. What is *scientia intuitiva?* In his earliest writings, Spinoza defined it simply as direct or immediate insight into a ratio or proportion. In his *Treatise on the Improvement of the Understanding* he said it is perceiving something through its essence. But in the *Ethics* he wrote that "it advances from an adequate idea of the formal essence of certain attributes of God to the adequate knowledge of the essence of things."[24] The attributes of God to which this definition refers are, of course, extension and thinking, and their formal (i.e. real) essence is that they express God's existence through *natura naturata*. Intuition is then direct and adequate knowledge of the unique and distinctive essence of something (ourselves, for instance) *as* an expression of God's activity. I mentioned earlier that in our emotions, particularly love, we sense and feel the characteristic existence of things as expressions of God. When we come to understand clearly and adequately that which earlier we sensed and felt, Spinoza calls this *scientia intuitiva*. In their perception of our own identity both imagination and intuition — the one felt obscurely the other seen clearly and adequately — are superior to reason.

According to Spinoza, it is because the mind is eternal that it can have intuitive knowledge and an intellectual love of God.[25] What is the connection between intuition, love, and eternity? First let's consider Spinoza's definition of eternity as "existence itself, so far as it is conceived necessarily to follow from the definition (i.e. the essence) alone of the eternal thing."[26] But you will remember, I hope, that this is also the definition of that which is self-caused and a free cause — that whose existence and action follows necessarily from its essence, that which cannot be conceived except as existing and acting. God's eternity, in brief, is synonymous with His freedom, His necessity, His infinity, and His absolute uniqueness. But if God's essence is the unbounded activity expressed throughout the universe, why should this be called *eternal?* The processes of nature are all temporal. Did Spinoza mean by *eternity* simply indefinite continuation through unlimited time? He denies that in the most emphatic terms. "Eternity cannot be defined by time or have any relationship to it."[27]

Spinoza's intention will be clearer if we examine quickly what he considered to be the contrast between time, duration and eternity. Both time and duration depend upon comparison. Time is a measuring rod, and duration is that which it measures. (In our daily speech we use "time" to cover both these senses.) Whether the units of time are the rotations of the earth or the decay of a radio-active atom, we take one rate of change as the basic unit in terms of which we count off other rates of change. By *duration,* Spinoza meant the order of succession in the continuing existence of anything, so that any period of its existence stands between what went before and what comes after. Even if duration were not measured by time, it would still require the comparison between what went before and what will come after any particular stretch of duration. Furthermore, this order of succession (earlier-later, or before-after) is the same throughout the existence of any one thing and across the existence of all things. Consequently, duration is abstract. The uniqueness of each moment is lost, and the differences between things and events are conflated. The comparison essential to both time and duration abstracts from the particularity of the individual thing that endures.

Eternity, on the other hand, is absolutely concrete and specific. It is the uniqueness of existence which admits of no possible comparison and no possible measure. Each thing is eternal, not as a node in a network, but as a singular mode through which flows a limitessly effervescent movement.[28] Most frequently we confuse eternity with immortality, and imagine it as an unending duration, filled with our memories and hopes. Eternity is not immortality, but neither is it the timeless abstract being of mathematical entities or Platonic Forms. Spinoza's conception is Biblical and Hebraic. It is the unrepeatable singularity which gives inner weight and significance to the incomparable story of Abraham and his silent journey with Isaac to Mt. Moriah and which Spinoza saw in all actually existing things and events. Each thing is, in its essence, its own singular species or form of God's eternity. This is what Spinoza meant by his famous phrase, *sub specie aeternitatis*. Strictly speaking, it is incorrect to say eternity is *now*, because this present moment is part of duration, the series of before and after. Eternity is not in time, but rather time is in eternity.

"We feel and know by experience that we are eternal."[29] We sense it in those culminating experiences of joy, of discovery, of love, of vibrant serenity, when we say to one another, "Let's hold on to this moment because it will never come again. It is precious beyond compare. Nothing like it has ever happened before." Such moments call for superlatives because comparatives cannot do them justice. Time comes to a stop, we say. Words fail us, because all words are general and fail to capture what is specific, what can never be repeated. But most of all, we sense eternity in the singularity and individuality of human beings. It is part of that revelation which shines through our daily lives in our sense of our own worth and in our poignant feeling for the immeasurable value of those we love.

"The intellectual love of God (*amor intellectuals Dei*) ... is eternal," Spinoza wrote,[30] because it arises from our clear and adequate understanding that in our primal libido and in our love for other human beings there is revealed also our love toward that necessary and incomparable existence which is God. Just as we can now see God expressing Himself in nature, and nature as existing in God, so too we can now understand clearly that in loving God we also love human beings, and in loving human beings we love God. The intellectual love of God is the union of the two precepts clearly taught by the Bible — love God, and love your neighbor.

To understand our love is not to abrogate it, or to turn it into pure thought purged of passion. Love and hate, anger and fear, yes, even fear of God, are necessary and irreducible aspects of human life. "A man is necessarily always subject to passions, and ... he follows and obeys the common order of nature...."[31] It is precisely for this reason that Spinoza scoffed at the traditional definition of man as a rational animal. Lev Shestov and Leo Strauss, along with many others, have attributed to Spinoza the belief that he showed the way to eliminate the passions and especially the fear of God. The first 22 propositions of Part IV of the *Ethics* are Spinoza's clear statement to the contrary. "It is above everything to be observed that the appetite by which a man is said to act is one and the same appetite as that by which he is said to suffer."[32] We cannot so much as wish to eliminate our passions entirely, since that would mean to cease to be a part of nature and to destroy ourselves[33]; and our essence is in self-affirming activity. When we act we form clear and adequate ideas. The essence of a human being is therefore *both* passion *and* clear understanding. We can, however, aim at increasing our power of acting and thus our clear understanding, recognizing at the same time that our understanding must always be limited by our passions. In particular, we can aim at attaining, as far as possible, that intellectual intuition which shows us how we ourselves, along with the rest of nature, are the expression of God.

Although we cannot hope to eliminate our emotions, we can control them. Spinoza pressed the analogy with our sensory illusions. When we come to understand the causes of some illusion — say, the twinkling of the distant stars — the image may remain unchanged but it has lost its power to mislead us. Similarly, when we understand clearly the causes of our love, fear, and anger these emotions do not disappear, but their power to control and dominate us is abated and, perhaps, destroyed. Even this power to control the emotions through knowledge, Spinoza suggested, is never complete. But the passions may become the smallest and least important part of the mind.

It follows then that the *amor intellectualis Dei* is not a cold unfeeling impassivity. It is a profound and deeply felt emotion which we control actively because we see clearly and adequately that in loving a human being we love God, and in loving God we love — indeed, God loves — human beings. In this understanding love our power of free action is increased, and this increase is joy, blessedness, and peace of mind. Just as Spinoza had earlier shown that *beneath* our hatred there is an underlying love and recognition of our human brotherhood, so too he believed he had demonstrated that *above* our fear of God we can always attain to an understanding love of God which can conquer our fear.

Does Spinoza promise us that we can actually achieve this *scientia intuitiva* and the eternity of the *amor intellectualis Dei?* In the *Treatise on the Improvement of the Understanding* he wrote, "The things which I have been able to know by this kind of knowledge are as yet very few."[34] Some years later, he concluded his *Ethics* with a line which echoes the Greek poets Hesiod and Simonides, "All noble things are as difficult as they are rare."[35]

FOOTNOTES

1. The letters are translated in A. Wolf, ed., *The Correspondence of Spinoza* (London, Allen and Unwin, 1928). References to the *Treatise on the Improvement of the Understanding* are to the Elwes translation, as reprinted in *Spinoza: Selections*, J. Wild, ed., (New York, Charles Scribner's Sons, 1930). References to the *Ethics* follow the abbreviations used by Professor A. Naess and his associates at the University of Oslo. The first number indicates the part or book of the *Ethics*. Abbreviations used are: P - Proposition, S - Scholium, C - Corollary, and Praef.-Preface. For Example, 2P3S refers to the scholium to Proposition 3 of Part 2. References to the *Tractatus Theologico-Politicus* are to the Elwes translation (New York, Dover Publications, Inc., 1951) and are abbreviated as T.T.-P.
2. 2P25.
3. 1P15.
4. 5P15.
5. Wild, *op. cit.*, p. 3.
6. 1P11.
7. Letter 54, to Boxel, 1674.
8. 4 Praef.
9. 2P3S.
10. 1P24.
11. 1P20.
12. 1P8S2.
13. 1P15.
14. Letter 50, to Jelles, 1674.
15. Letter 58, to Schuller, 1674.
16. 2P43S.
17. 2P17S.
18. Letter 17, to Balling, 1664.
19. 4P68S.

20. T.T.-P., ch. 12, p. 172.
21. 2P37.
22. 4P4.
23. 4P7.
24. 2P40C2.
25. 5P31, 5P33.
26. 1P8.
27. 5P23S.
28. 2P45S.
29. 5P23S.
30. 5P33.
31. 4P4C.
32. 5P4S.
33. 3P8, 3P9.
34. Wild, *op. cit.*, p. 8.
35 5P42S.

CONCLUDING REMARKS
Eugene Mihaly[*]

The familiar statement of Rabbi Yohanan in the name of Rabbi Simeon bar Yohai may serve as a fitting coda to these proceedings:

> Whenever students repeat the teachings of a deceased scholar, his lips gently move (*dovevot*) in the grave (*Yevamot* 97a).

Our intent in arranging this series of Efroymson Memorial Lectures on Spinoza was to pay homage to one of the giant intellects of modern times, to highlight the many facets of Spinoza's thought — to hear again, calling from the grave, as it were, his gentle whisper. Our purpose was to explore and, from the perspective of three centuries, to evaluate Spinoza's contribution and lasting influence and to bring to the attention of the academic and broader community the special affinity of the Hebrew Union College and Reform Judaism to this seminal mind.

Notwithstanding his alienation from the Jewish community in his own lifetime, in spite of Spinoza's excommunication and his negative (or as Hermann Cohen would term it, "vindictive") judgment of his ancestral faith — especially in the *Tractatus* — Spinoza played a unique role in the intellectual development of countless Jews as they struggled to enter and cope with a post-medieval world — from Mendelssohn to our own day.

One of the aims of Mendelssohn's first work, *The Philosophical Dialogues*, was the rehabilitation of Spinoza. Far from considering him an outcast, Mendelssohn was fascinated

---
[*]Dr. Eugene Mihaly is Professor of Rabbinic Literature and Homiletics and Executive Dean for Academic Affairs of HUC-JIR.

by him. "Despite his speculative doctrine, Spinoza could have remained an Orthodox Jew...," Mendelssohn writes (*Gesammelte Schriften* 3:5, cf. A. Altmann, *Moses Mendelssohn*, pp. 33ff.). More significantly, however, in his interpretation of the revelation at Sinai as consisting of a series of commandments rather than "eternal truths," Mendelssohn followed Spinoza. Mendelssohn thus disseminated and lent his authority and prestige to an interpretation of Judaism which at least in part was Spinozistic. This had far reaching consequences not only with Jewish circles, but perhaps even more importantly, in terms of the way Judaism was perceived by the broader intellectual community — by Kant and his followers, among numerous others.

Altmann suggests that Mendelssohn "may even have dreamt of becoming a 'second Spinoza'...." (*ibid.* p. 34). Myriads of incipient young philosophers in the *yeshivot* of Central and Eastern Europe as well as in the United States shared this "dream." Spinoza served as a half-way house, as Professor Feuer so aptly phrased it, on their road to westernization and in their struggle to free themselves from the obscurantism, the dogmatism, and even tyranny of an encrusted tradition.

The relationship of the Hebrew Union College and Reform Judaism to Spinoza flows from the essence of liberal religion which we espouse and to which we have been historically committed. The tangible evidence of this kinship is our great collection of Spinozana housed in the Klau Library and is manifest in our objective study of religious texts and in our devotion to the spirit of free inquiry. We are Spinoza's heirs in our firm resolve to combat every form of obscurantism and fundamentalism.

We have indeed heard Spinoza's voice in the lectures by our distinguished guests, Professors Feuer, Popkin and Savan, and in the stimulating discussions at each session. Spinoza's lips moved during these past two days. On behalf of our entire academic community, we express our deep gratitude to our guest lecturers for their outstanding contribution, to our faculty committee, Dean Ehrlich, Professors Kogan, Paper, Rivkin, and Zafren, who made all the arrangements for this event and who chaired the various sessions. Our President, Dr. Alfred Gottschalk, who conceived of the project, merits a special word of appreciation. It was due to his deep interest and encouragement that this significant event took place.

Finally, in the spirit of the talmudic admonition that when we part from friends we should do so with words of Torah (see *Berakhot* 31a), I conclude with two citations — one from the Midrash and one from Spinoza:

> Why is the Holy One, blessed be He, called "Place"? Because He is the place of the world, but the world is not his place.
> *Genesis Rabbah* LXVIII.II, ed. Theodor, p. 777.

> Whatever is, is in God, and without God nothing can be or be conceived.
> *The Ethics*, Part I, Prop. XV.